WINE
MONDAYS

WINE

MONDAYS

simple wine pairings
with seasonal menus

FROM THE JAMES BEARD AWARD–WINNING
PROPRIETOR OF L'ESPALIER AND SEL DE LA TERRE

FRANK McCLELLAND
AND CHRISTIE MATHESON

The Harvard Common Press

BOSTON, MASSACHUSETTS

The Harvard Common Press
535 Albany Street
Boston, Massachusetts 02118
www.harvardcommonpress.com

Printed in the United States of America
Printed on acid-free paper

Library of Congress Cataloging-in-Publication Data
McClelland, Frank.
  Wine Mondays : simple wine pairings with seasonal menus / Frank
McClelland and Christie Matheson.
      p. cm.
    Includes index.
    ISBN-13: 978-1-55832-377-3 (hardcover : alk. paper)
  1. Cookery. 2. Wine and wine making. 3. Menus. I. Matheson, Christie. II.
Title.
  TX714.M379255 2008
  641.5--dc22   2008003497

Special bulk-order discounts are available on this and other Harvard Common
Press books. Companies and organizations may purchase books for premiums or
resale, or may arrange a custom edition, by contacting the Marketing Director at
the address above.

Book design by Matthew Bouloutian and Vivian Ghazarian

Jacket and interior photographs by White/Packert
Food styling by Frank McClelland and James Hackney
Prop styling by Katrine Kelly
except for front jacket, far left (Pomegranate and Goat Cheese Salad)
Photograph © 2008 by Eskite Photography
Food styling by Andrea Lucich; prop styling by Carol Hacker

10 9 8 7 6 5 4 3 2 1

TO MY CHILDREN, WHO GIVE ME A REASON TO COOK EVERY DAY

F. K. M.

CONTENTS

ACKNOWLEDGMENTS

It is quite a daunting task to thank all of the people who have influenced this seemingly simple approach of menus built around food and wine.

I want to thank Christie Matheson for her help in making this book a reality. She is a true inspiration to me, always positive, always pushing me to do my best.

Thank you to Erik Johnson, my wine buyer and teacher, for being the personality behind Wine Mondays at L'Espalier. Erik is the inspiration for the food and wine combinations, and I have enjoyed all of the bottles of wine that we've drunk together in search of that perfect match.

A thank-you to the team at The Harvard Common Press—Valerie Cimino, Virginia Downes, and Jane Dornbusch, who made sure we got it right by asking all the right questions. And thanks to our agent, Stacey Glick, for help throughout this process.

Thanks to the colleagues of mine who give me inspiration every day in the way of food, wine, service, and love of the people who come through the doors of L'Espalier and Sel de la Terre. The close-knit family that represents our restaurant group brings me joy and support through its dedication to and pursuit of my philosophy that "only the best is good enough." In particular, thank you to Chef Geoff Gardner, Chef James Hackney, Louis Risoli, Chef Daniel Bojorquez, Chef Louis DiBiccari, Chef B.J. Salazar, Fernando da Silva, and all my other colleagues through the years who have contributed to this work. Special thanks to Nick Tranquillo, my quirky, genius sidekick.

For Kris Rodammer's friendship and vision through graphics, colors, and art, thank you.

Thanks to all the farmers in New England who have inspired my 30-year career and give reason to what I do every day.

Thanks must go out to my grandparents, Foster and Virginia McClelland, who inspired me with their Garden of Eden and all that was good in life.

Thanks to my four children, Keppler, Annie, James, and Olivia. They are the joys of my life. And thanks to my yellow Lab, Lance Seawater McClelland, who goes everywhere with me.

Enormous thanks to my wife, Heather, who teaches me every day that nothing is too difficult. She brings peace to my heart with everything she does.

—F.K.M.

Most of all, thanks to Frank McClelland—brilliant, talented, creative, generous, a little bit crazy, always funny—for giving me the opportunity to work on such a fantastic project. L'Espalier is a magical place, and I am thrilled to have helped with the creation of this book. Thanks to Erik Johnson, L'Espalier's extraordinary wine director, for sharing his encyclopedic knowledge (along with quite a few tastes) of wine and for consistently cracking me up. Thanks to our agent, Stacey Glick, who loved this idea from the very beginning. Thanks to Valerie Cimino for being a wonderful editor and a super-savvy foodie. Thanks to everyone at The Harvard Common Press for taking such excellent care of *Wine Mondays*. Thanks to Lorin Seidman, my fabulous food-loving friend, for getting this book started. Thanks to the entire team at L'Espalier for being unfailingly gracious, fun, and never, ever pretentious. They are a rare group in the world of exquisite restaurants. And, of course, thanks forever and always to my two very favorite people to have dinner with: my brother, Seth Matheson, and my love, my husband (!), Will Adams.

—C.M.

INTRODUCTION

L'Espalier is an elegant restaurant located in Boston's Back Bay neighborhood, and I have owned it since 1988. Our food is inspired by the classic techniques of French cooking and the produce, meats, and artisanal cheeses of New England. We work with ingredients that are the freshest, in season, and abundant. We seek out the best-quality ingredients we can find, and when possible we purchase foods that are locally available and organic.

My philosophy about fresh ingredients dates back to my early childhood. I grew up with my grandparents on their farm in the White Mountains of New Hampshire. We all helped harvest vegetables, collect eggs, and prepare meals with the bounty from our farm and nearby farms. I learned from my grandmother that fresh, local, seasonal ingredients are the best—and I have insisted upon using them as much as possible throughout my professional cooking career. I always advise home cooks to work with ingredients that are readily available—so please do not feel bound by every last ingredient in the recipes in this book. If a particular item isn't in season, of sufficient quality, or available in your local market, substitute something else. And as you cook, remember that the meal would not exist without the producer of the ingredients. Get to know, and support, your local farmers by visiting local vegetable stands and farmers' markets regularly. I guarantee that you will be glad you did, and your cooking will be better for it.

Though L'Espalier is known as a special-occasion restaurant—more marriage proposals take place in our dining room than in any other restaurant in Boston—we aim to be relaxed and friendly while providing exquisite service that makes our guests feel special. And we love to let our hair down and have fun. That's one of the reasons why in 2002 L'Espalier's wine director, Erik Johnson, and I started our Wine Mondays program, which is the inspiration for this book.

We host Wine Mondays every Monday night (unless it's a major holiday or the restaurant is closed for some reason), and it's a fun and relaxed way to start the week. Guests come in and enjoy open seating (so they can meet new people and perhaps make new friends) and a four-course meal with wines at each course, all centered around a theme (such as Burgundy, Italy, sparkling wine, and even occasions like Halloween). Erik Johnson is the most entertaining wine director in town, and he leads the educational component of the evening, talking briefly about each wine and how and why it pairs well with certain foods. So our guests learn something, and usually laugh quite a bit in the process. The food on Wine Mondays isn't quite as complicated as the food we serve on our regular menu (which changes nightly according to what's fresh)—and our guests always rave about it.

Wine Mondays has always been affordably priced—as of this writing it's just $60 for all four courses and their accompanying wines—and that's part of its *raison d'être*. We want this night to be as accessible as possible and to encourage people who haven't visited us to come on in and get to know us.

For this book, we selected 16 of our favorite Wine Mondays menus from recent years, four from each season, and we present them here along with information about the wines we paired with each of the courses. These are the actual wines we chose when we served these menus at L'Espalier, and some of the menus are from a year or two ago. This is why you'll notice a range of vintages, and some of the older bottles may no longer be available. Therefore, we always offer suggestions in the Wine Notes sections for finding other good wines to try with each dish. Of course, we love the winemakers we work with and encourage you to seek out their products (even if you buy a later vintage) so that you can try them and see what you think.

Because we hope you will use this book when entertaining friends and family, each menu and all the recipes are set up with a dinner party in mind: four (not-too-big) courses all serving six people. (Note: If you are hosting a dinner for six people, plan to have a bottle of wine for each course so that everyone gets a generous taste of each wine. Of course, it's never a bad idea to have extra wine on hand.)

You probably won't be throwing a dinner party every night, so please also use the recipes here for more casual entertaining or everyday cooking. If you want to choose just one or two menu items to serve as your meal, then you can plan on each recipe feeding two to four people nicely. Having four courses for six people is merely a guideline.

Which brings me to an important point: Don't feel compelled to do everything that I recommend in this book. I hope that you feel free to use your creativity in the kitchen. This book is meant to inspire and motivate you, not to make you feel stressed out about obtaining every single ingredient and cooking every single thing. If you don't have the time to make every single component of a dish, that's fine. You will see as you read through the recipes that many involve multiple elements, and in many cases just using one or two of the elements is perfectly sufficient. Of course, if you do have time to do it all, trust me, the results will be amazing.

Remember, this book is a tool, not a set of hard and fast rules. The recipes are easy to follow and understand, and explain clearly how to use many intriguing ingredients and techniques that I hope you'll want to try, even if you've never tried them before. I've spent decades in the kitchen, and I want you to have an increased appreciation and love of the art of cooking, so I am passing along my knowledge to you—do with it what you will. And have fun!

MIXING AND MATCHING FOOD AND WINE

All of the menus in this book are intended to serve six people as a four-course meal. However, you may not want to prepare all four courses for a particular meal. You may opt to make only two or three of the courses in any given menu, and in that case, the amounts of food will work well for three to four people.

In addition, feel free to experiment and devise your own menus by pulling one course from one menu in the book, and the other courses from different menus. If you create your own menus, try to choose recipes that feature ingredients in season—and in general try not to have similar ingredients in all the courses. A variety of flavors stimulates the palate and makes for exciting eating. A good guideline is that, for a four-course meal, the first course should be the simplest and lightest (maybe a salad or soup), with a second course that's a little heavier, like seafood or poultry. The third course should be the heartiest—think red meat, game, or a hearty stew—and then you can wind down with something sweet or a small cheese course. You can also plan menus around your favorite wines. If you have four wines you want to serve, try to serve them in order from lightest to heaviest (finishing with something sweet), and choose dishes to pair with them accordingly.

Even if you're planning to serve only two or three courses from different menus, keep flavors, ingredients, and richness in mind. For example, if you want to start with Pan-Roasted Black Bass with Shrimp Flan and Stir-Fried Shiitakes (page 44), your next course could be Crispy Confit Duck Hash with Black Kale and Poached Eggs (page 57). The bass is lighter, and is a good prelude to the richer duck. Or you could follow the bass with Barbecued Chicken with Grilled Ramps and Blue Potato Salad (page 92), which—like the bass—is somewhat Asian-inspired, and is rich and intensely flavorful. On the other hand, if you aren't interested in the bass and want to start with the duck (a rich dish), you wouldn't want to serve, say, Walnut-Encrusted Spring Lamb with Bacon-Potato Rösti (page 82) as the next course. You'd need a richer and more intense course to follow the duck, because your palate will have been too stimulated to enjoy the delicate flavors of the lamb. Something like Sautéed Shrimp with Brown Sugar, Chili-Glazed Pink Grapefruit, and Citrus Hollandaise (page 26) would be a better follow-up to the duck.

INGREDIENTS

Throughout this book you'll find information on many specific ingredients in the recipes, but there are some ingredients that appear again and again. Here are my preferences for some key kitchen staples; unless otherwise specified, these are what I suggest you use.

Salt: When I mention salt in a recipe, I always mean sea salt, unless I specifically say otherwise. Sea salt has the natural mineral flavors of the ocean. It's milder yet more flavorful than standard table salt. I encourage cooks to experiment with different kinds of sea salt when cooking at home. If I give a specific measurement for salt, I recommend starting with that—you can always add more, but it's tough to remove saltiness from an oversalted dish. If a recipe just says "salt" with no measurement, season with salt to your taste.

Pepper: Unless specified otherwise, I mean freshly ground black pepper. Sometimes I use white pepper, which should also be freshly ground. There's no reason not to have two inexpensive pepper mills in your spice cabinet, one for black pepper and one for white. As with salt, if I include a specific measurement, start with that and add more if desired. If it just says "pepper," season with freshly ground black pepper to taste.

Herbs: Unless I specify dried herbs, I always suggest using fresh. I like the instant intensity and the natural oils that fresh herbs give off, and their true herbal flavor. You never know how long dried herbs have been on the shelf, and they can lose fragrance quickly. You can substitute dried for fresh, though—just use about half as much dried as you would fresh.

Butter: I always use unsalted butter. Salted butter varies in its salinity, and using unsalted butter means you control the level of salt in a dish. I love organic butter from Vermont—and it's more widely available than ever.

Leeks: I love cooking with leeks, as you will see, and I encourage you to use leeks more often. They have a wonderful, subtle flavor. Use them with onions in soups, sauces, marinades, and more. Make them part of your regular repertoire. In my house we never prepare a *mirepoix* (traditionally a sautéed mixture of onions, carrots, and celery) without a leek.

Oils: You don't need to use the very best olive oil for everything. In my kitchen I use vegetable oil for sautéing and a good (but not super-expensive) olive oil for making pestos, tapenades, and tomato sauce, and for some sautéing. I also always have on hand a top-of-the-line, first-cold-pressing extra virgin olive oil from Italy, Spain, or California that I reserve for vinaigrettes or to finish a soup. (High-end extra virgin olive oils, if you're not using them up within a month of being opened, should be refrigerated, or they could go rancid.) And I keep grapeseed oil on hand, mostly for super-high-temperature sautéing. It's okay to use vegetable oil, but grapeseed oil, which has become more readily available, works especially well because it has a high burning point. Also, research shows that grapeseeds contain healthy antioxidants.

EQUIPMENT

The recipes in this book call for a variety of kitchen equipment. You don't need to own every culinary gadget, and you can often improvise. But here are a few items I think are very important to have in your kitchen.

Sauté pans: Have at least three sizes of sauté pans (small, medium-size, and large), because one size does not fit all. If you're sautéing a piece of meat or fish and it's as big as your sauté pan, it will steam instead of caramelizing and sautéing properly. If it's much smaller than your pan, it could burn before it sautés properly. Fit the pan to what you're cooking.

Wooden spoons: I like to use wooden spoons to stir things in pans. If you're stirring something that's caramelized you won't scrape the burnt portions off the pan—just the good parts. Even high-quality wooden spoons are relatively inexpensive, so I recommend you keep several of varying handle lengths and bowl sizes.

Knives: Purchase the best knives that you can find; the investment will pay off. Keep your knives as sharp as possible. Maintain them by bringing them to a knife store and having the edges beveled every 6 months, ideally. And sharpen them at home on a steel, at a 45-degree angle, every time you use them.

Pepper grinder: You should always have a pepper grinder (or ideally two—one for black pepper and one for white pepper) by your side in the kitchen so that freshly ground pepper is always at hand. Look for grinders with different coarseness settings so you have the option of finely ground and coarsely ground.

TECHNIQUES

Throughout the book, I describe a variety of cooking techniques in sidebars located near the recipes to which they pertain. But there are a few techniques that I use again and again.

Preheating pans: You will notice that I often suggest heating pans on the stove burners before adding oil or butter to them. Heating the pan first by itself helps foods stick to the pan less, and when you add your oil or butter it will heat more evenly and completely, all at once. However, do not preheat nonstick skillets this way—the chemical coating could release unhealthy fumes.

Making marinades: Many recipes in this book call for preparing marinades for meats, fish, and vegetables. Though the marinades themselves are simple to make, the marinating process takes extra time, and often requires starting a recipe in advance, but it's worth it. Marinades can enhance flavor, develop character, and add moistness like nothing else.

Manipulating heat: The recipes in this book often call for adjusting the cooking temperature by turning the heat up and down. This is for a good reason. Don't be afraid to adjust your heat source constantly. Off and high are not the only two settings. Watch your food, learn how it responds to heat, and manipulate the heat to get the best results. Each oven and stovetop is different, so get to know yours, watch your heat, and work it. This is a skill that you will easily develop the more you cook.

WINE

For each menu in this book, we tell you which wines we chose to accompany the food when we served it during a Wine Mondays dinner at the restaurant. The wines are from dozens of different grape varieties and regions, and we hope you'll discover something new as you read. We also suggest some alternative wines so that you don't have to go on a wild goose chase for a specific bottle—unless you want to. Before you get started, though, here are a few general things about wine to keep in mind.

Drink What You Like

Above all else, remember that it's not life and death. It's just dinner and wine. Eat what you like to eat, and drink what you like to drink. If you like something, who's to say you're wrong? The wines we describe in this book are just suggestions. Try all kinds of different wines from all over the world to learn about what you love best.

Pair Thoughtfully

Hey, if you like a big Cabernet Sauvignon with a delicate seafood starter, go for it. But in general, it's a good idea to have the weight of the wine complement the weight of the food. Lighter foods shouldn't be overpowered by a heavy wine, and robust dishes don't benefit from being paired with something so subtle it's barely there. For example, we served a minerally Sauvignon de Saint-Bris with the summery Skillet-Roasted Sea Bass with Watermelon Broth (page 135), but I would not choose that wine to go with the richer Pot-Roasted Pork with Chorizo and Clams (page 73). Nor would I recommend the fruity-yet-earthy Cabernet Sauvignon paired with Grilled Rib-Eye Steaks with Frank's Potato Gratin (page 115) to go with Oysters on the Half Shell with Seaweed Salad, Sherry Mignonette, and Caviar (page 79). (But again, if you think those pairings taste delicious, why not drink them?) There's a give-and-take between food and wine, so try to work with what's happening on the plate when choosing the wine to serve. Also, be sure to try the wine, then taste the food, then try the wine and food again to see how the flavors change. That's the cool part!

Also consider the time of year when planning your menu and your wine. When it's cold out, a crisp Sauvignon Blanc doesn't necessarily appeal . . . and when it's hot, who wants a thick, earthy red? But remember, Champagne goes with everything at any time of year. So do most dry rosés.

Opposites Sometimes Attract

While you might want to match the weight of your food and wine, the complexity of the two can be a different story. If you have a complex dish with tons of flavors going on, you don't want the wine to compete; you want a simpler choice. (Case in point: the Seviche of Striped Bass with Lime-Cucumber Salsa on page 113, which has a lot of flavors melding together, is nicely complemented by a straightforward Chenin Blanc.) And if you have a complex wine, it might taste best with simpler food. (A basic roast chicken, for example, can be outstanding with a nuanced bottle of Burgundy.)

Take the Temperature

Drink wine at the right temperature. Most restaurants, and many people at home, serve the whites too cold and the reds too warm. Doing so means you'll taste lots of alcohol and not much else. Whites should be slightly cool to the touch (45° to 48°F), and reds should be a little under room temperature (65° to 68°F). If you must err, err on the side of too cool.

Keep red wine in a cool, dark place (ideally a small air-conditioned room). If you open a bottle and don't finish it, yes, you can put it in the refrigerator—just bring it back up almost to room temperature before you serve it again.

For whites, chill them in the refrigerator for a few hours before serving, and take them out about 20 minutes before you plan to pour them. Keep them on the table, not on ice, while you're eating. If you don't finish a bottle of white, recork it and store it in the refrigerator, where it should last for a couple of days.

Be Glassy

You don't need to invest in different glasses for every kind of wine. Medium-size wineglasses are the first thing you should buy—they can be all-purpose. If you can't find a wineglass labeled "all-purpose," look for wineglasses on the larger size. But not huge! Too-large glasses—those with tons of volume that could seemingly hold half a bottle of wine or more—mean your nose will be too far from the bouquet and you'll miss some of the flavor. Bigger red wines need more space to breathe, though, which is why glasses for red wine tend to be bigger than glasses for white wine.

By the way, the breathing doesn't have to happen in the glass: Don't be afraid to decant your red wine! There are many beautiful wine decanters for sale, or you could use a simple glass pitcher. Pouring wine out of the bottle into a decanter frees the wine from any sediment at the bottom of the bottle, and helps to aerate it to lessen the impact of tannins. Younger red wines especially benefit from the oxidation that occurs when you decant—it gives the wine a little more "age" and rounds out the flavor. If you don't drink all the decanted wine, you can pour it back into the bottle—if there's no sediment in there (don't wash the bottle to get rid of sediment, because residual water can dilute the wine)—and recork it, or you can cover your decanter tightly with plastic wrap and keep it in the fridge for a couple of days.

Be adventurous! And remember—we'll say it again—drink what you like. Cheers!

SWEET SENDOFF

When we host Wine Mondays at L'Espalier, we always send guests home with a little treat to enjoy later, or to share with someone who couldn't be there. The perennial favorites are our macaroons and our cannelés.

L'Espalier Macaroons MAKES ABOUT 2 DOZEN

These simple cookies are surprisingly satisfying, but not too cloying or rich to follow a meal.

1 cup condensed milk

1 large egg white

1¼ teaspoons pure vanilla extract

Pinch of salt

1 pound (about 6 cups) shredded sweetened coconut

1 Preheat the oven to 325°F. Line baking sheets with parchment paper.

2 In a large bowl, whisk together the condensed milk, egg white, vanilla, and salt.

3 Working in batches, pulse the coconut in a food processor for 15 seconds, until the coconut pieces are similar in size to grains of rice. Add the coconut to the condensed milk mixture and thoroughly incorporate by hand. Roll into 1-inch balls and place on the parchment-lined baking sheets.

4 Bake for 12 minutes, rotating the sheets after 6 minutes. Remove to a wire rack to cool. Store in an airtight container for up to 5 days.

L'Espalier Cannelés

These little French pastries—something between a beignet and a custard—are at once moist and airy, and are just sweet enough to satisfy. Look for cannelé molds in specialty kitchen shops or online. You can also bake the pastries in mini muffin tins.

2 tablespoons butter, plus
   more for the molds

1 cup milk

2 large eggs

1 large egg yolk

½ teaspoon pure vanilla extract

½ teaspoon rum

½ cup all-purpose flour

1 cup sugar

¼ teaspoon salt

1 Combine the butter and milk in a small saucepan over low heat until the butter has melted. Stir to distribute the butter evenly in the milk. In a medium-size bowl, combine the eggs, egg yolk, vanilla, and rum. In a large bowl, whisk together the flour, sugar, and salt. Whisk the egg mixture into the flour mixture, then whisk in the warm milk mixture.

2 Strain the batter through a fine-mesh sieve and let it sit at room temperature for 1 hour. Cover and refrigerate overnight.

3 Preheat the oven to 400°F.

4 Butter the cannelé molds and fill them three-quarters full with batter. Bake for 1 hour. Let cool on a wire rack before unmolding. Store in an airtight container for up to 3 days.

WINTER

BUBBLES, BUBBLES EVERYWHERE!

Sparkling wine is fantastic with all kinds of food. When in doubt, pair a dish with a sparkler. Sparkling wines generally have more acidity than table wine, and that makes them a perfect palate cleanser—it's like a little sorbet course in a glass. When eating, the first few bites are often the most flavorful, and then proteins and fats build up on your tongue and dull subsequent flavors a bit. But the effervescent acidity of sparkling wine clears the palate so that the last bite can be as tasty as the first.

WINTER → Bubbles, Bubbles Everywhere!

MENU
& pairings
↓

 +

PAIRINGS

Roasted Beet, Baby Arugula, and Orange Salad with Blini and Caviar Crème Fraîche

1

Louis Bouillot, "Grande Réserve," Brut, Crémant de Bourgogne, Burgundy, France

Forest Mushroom Risotto with Broccoli Rabe

2

Beaumont des Crayères, "Grand Prestige," Brut, Champagne, France

Poached Guinea Hens in Champagne with Baby Bok Choy

3

1996 Westport Rivers, "Cuvée L'Espalier," Brut, Westport, Massachusetts

Pain Perdu with Roasted Pears and Honey-Thyme Apricots

4

2005 Beppe Marino, "Muray," Moscato d'Asti, Piedmont, Italy

WINE NOTES

↓

1ST PAIRING **ROASTED BEET, BABY ARUGULA, AND ORANGE SALAD WITH BLINI AND CAVIAR CRÈME FRAÎCHE**
SERVED WITH → **LOUIS BOUILLOT, "GRANDE RÉSERVE," BRUT, CRÉMANT DE BOURGOGNE, BURGUNDY, FRANCE**

When you're trying four kinds of sparkling wine in one evening, it's fun to get bottles from several different countries. It's not just about Champagne, even when it comes to French bubbly. This is a light, crisp sparkling wine made from the same grape varieties and using the exact same method as Champagne, but it's produced in Burgundy. If you get French sparkling wine from beyond the borders of Champagne, the price tends to go down—and there are plenty of great bottles to be found. Since we are doing a slight twist on traditional Champagne, we've also done a twist on one of the most traditional foods to pair with Champagne—caviar. The tart, racy flavors of this wine are great with the sweet roasted beets, too.

2ND PAIRING **FOREST MUSHROOM RISOTTO WITH BROCCOLI RABE**
SERVED WITH → **BEAUMONT DES CRAYÈRES, "GRAND PRESTIGE," BRUT, CHAMPAGNE, FRANCE**

Yes, we have included one wine from Champagne. This one's a real classic, and Beaumont is a small Champagne house that harvests all the grapes by hand, so the quality is very high. But you could try another dry Champagne with this dish, and enjoy the acidity and crispness with the earthy mushrooms and the creamy risotto.

3RD PAIRING **POACHED GUINEA HENS IN CHAMPAGNE WITH BABY BOK CHOY**
SERVED WITH → **1996 WESTPORT RIVERS, "CUVÉE L'ESPALIER," BRUT, WESTPORT, MASSACHUSETTS**

Westport is a small Massachusetts vineyard producing wonderful high-quality sparkling wine. This particular vintage was created just for us at L'Espalier, but you can find other fantastic Westport bruts. Because we do so much cooking with local ingredients, we love to serve local wines when we can. Explore your region to discover what quality wines are being produced near you—there are wineries all over the United States, in places you might not expect!

4TH PAIRING **PAIN PERDU WITH ROASTED PEARS AND HONEY-THYME APRICOTS**
SERVED WITH → **2005 BEPPE MARINO, "MURAY," MOSCATO D'ASTI, PIEDMONT, ITALY**

Moscato d'Asti is just a little bit sweet and just a little bit effervescent, what the Italians call *frizzante*. This one is wonderfully balanced, with the flavor of biting into a ripe peach or apricot, and it tastes fantastic with a fruit dessert. It's low in alcohol, which makes it a nice way to end a meal.

Roasted Beet, Baby Arugula, and Orange Salad with Blini and Caviar Crème Fraîche

This is a beautiful salad, contrasting sweet, colorful beets with somewhat bitter green arugula and tangy orange segments. You may use any kind of caviar you like. Sparkling wine plays well off all the flavors on the plate. The blini also make great Sunday morning pancakes. Sometimes I stir finely chopped vegetables into the batter and serve the blinis as a side dish with poultry.

2 bunches (about 1½ pounds) small beets (mixed golden and red if possible), scrubbed, leaves removed, and ends trimmed

3 tablespoons vegetable oil

1 teaspoon dried oregano

2 teaspoons salt

1 bunch baby arugula

1 tablespoon fresh lemon juice

2 tablespoons olive oil

Freshly ground black pepper

1 orange, cut into sections (page 27)

1 Preheat the oven to 375°F.

2 Toss the beets with the vegetable oil, oregano, and 1 teaspoon of the salt. Place them in a roasting pan and roast for 45 minutes to 1 hour, until a knife can pierce the thickest portion of the beet with minimal resistance.

3 Remove the beets from the oven and let cool for 20 to 25 minutes, until they are warm, not hot, to the touch. Peel the skin off the beets (the skins should rub off easily). Slice the beets into wedges. In a large bowl, toss the beets with the arugula, lemon juice, olive oil, the remaining 1 teaspoon salt, and pepper. Add the orange segments to the bowl and gently toss again.

4 To serve, spoon 1 tablespoon Caviar Crème Fraîche (page 14) onto each of 6 plates. Place 3 warm Blini (page 14) on each plate next to the crème fraîche, and divide the salad evenly among the plates, placing a pile of salad next to the blini.

Caviar Crème Fraîche

¾ cup crème fraîche (page 74)

1 tablespoon fresh lemon juice

Zest of 1 lemon

1 ounce American caviar of your
    choice

1 tablespoon fresh chervil

¼ teaspoon cayenne pepper

Mix the crème fraîche, lemon juice and zest, caviar, chervil, and cayenne together in a small bowl until thoroughly combined. You can make this 2 to 3 hours ahead and keep it in the refrigerator. Remove it from the refrigerator 15 to 20 minutes before you're ready to serve.

Blini

1 cup all-purpose flour

¼ cup buckwheat flour

1 heaping teaspoon baking
    powder

½ teaspoon salt

½ teaspoon sugar

1 large egg

1 cup buttermilk or whole milk

2 tablespoons plain yogurt

1 tablespoon vegetable oil

1 tablespoon butter

1 Preheat the oven to 200°F.

2 Sift together the flours, baking powder, salt, and sugar in a large bowl. In a separate bowl, beat together the egg, buttermilk, yogurt, and vegetable oil. Slowly pour the wet ingredient mixture into the dry ingredients, whisking until fully incorporated.

3 Place a large skillet over medium heat for about 3 minutes. Add the butter. When the butter is sizzling, turn the heat down to medium-low. Spoon silver dollar–size dollops of batter into the skillet. Cook for 2 minutes, turn the blini over, and cook for 1 more minute.

4 Move the blini from the skillet to a sheet pan and place them in the oven to keep warm until ready to serve.

Forest Mushroom Risotto
with Broccoli Rabe

This vegetarian course is creamy and decadent, and the mushrooms give it a deep, almost meaty flavor. Placing a few stems of broccoli rabe on top of each serving of risotto provides a contrast in flavors and textures.

1 cup dried mixed mushrooms (such as cèpes, black trumpets, chanterelles, or hedgehogs)

2 cups hot water

2 tablespoons olive oil

1 cup diced yellow onion

1 cup Arborio rice

4 garlic cloves, minced

1 cup Champagne or sparkling wine

1½ cups vegetable broth

1½ cups freshly grated Parmesan cheese

1 cup heavy cream

4 tablespoons kosher salt

½ teaspoon freshly ground white pepper

2 tablespoons fresh lemon juice

1 tablespoon white truffle oil

1 Place the mushrooms in a medium-size bowl and pour the hot water over them. Let stand for 25 minutes, until the mushrooms are rehydrated.

2 Heat the oil in a medium-size heavy saucepan on medium-high heat for 1 minute. Add the onion and sauté until translucent, about 3 minutes. Reduce the heat to medium and add the rice. Sauté the rice for 3 to 4 minutes, stirring frequently.

3 Drain and slice the mushrooms, and add them to the pan. Cook for about 2 minutes, then add the garlic and cook for 15 seconds. Turn the heat back up to medium-high and add the Champagne, stirring constantly with a wooden spoon, until the liquid is absorbed, 2 to 3 minutes. Add the vegetable broth, about ½ cup at a time, stirring constantly after each addition until the liquid is absorbed. Repeat this process until you have used all the broth.

4 Stir in the cheese, cream, salt, pepper, lemon juice, and truffle oil. Cook for another 3 to 5 minutes, stirring frequently, until the rice is *al dente*. The total cooking time should be 25 to 28 minutes. The consistency of the risotto should not be too thick—if necessary, add more vegetable broth and cream in equal proportion to achieve a looser texture. Serve immediately with the Broccoli Rabe (page 16).

Broccoli Rabe

1 tablespoon salt, plus more for
    seasoning

1 bunch broccoli rabe (about
    ½ pound), 1 inch trimmed from
    the base of the stems

1 tablespoon butter

1 garlic clove, minced

Freshly ground black pepper

1 Fill a large pot halfway with water, and add 1 tablespoon salt. Bring to a boil over high heat. Add the broccoli rabe to the boiling water and cook for 4 minutes.

2 Remove the broccoli rabe from the water and plunge it into ice water to stop the cooking process. Remove it from the ice water.

3 Heat a small sauté pan over medium-high heat for 2 minutes. Add the butter. When the butter is sizzling, add the garlic and the broccoli rabe and sauté for 3 to 4 minutes. Season with salt and pepper to taste.

Poached Guinea Hens
in Champagne with Baby Bok Choy

A guinea hen has a sweet, gamey taste—it contains all the flavor that I wish a fresh turkey had. I think it's delicious with Champagne. This is a simple dish that can be made mostly ahead of time. You can do everything up to reheating it in the skillet and roasting it in the oven a day in advance; keep it covered in the refrigerator until you're ready to sear and roast. Look for guinea hens at your local butcher shop.

3 tablespoons grapeseed oil

5 tablespoons butter

Two 2-pound guinea hens,
    legs removed and back cut out
    (page 18)

1 yellow onion, chopped

2 carrots, peeled and chopped

1 leek, washed (page 195)
    and chopped

2 celery stalks, chopped

4 garlic cloves, crushed

1 whole clove

1 teaspoon whole fennel seeds

2 teaspoons dried thyme

2 bay leaves

1 teaspoon dried tarragon

½ cup sherry

1½ cups Champagne or
    sparkling wine

2 quarts chicken or vegetable
    broth

12 stalks baby bok choy

Salt and freshly ground black
    pepper

1   Place a large pot over medium-high heat. Add the oil and 2 tablespoons of the butter and heat for about 3 minutes. Add the hen legs, breasts, and backs to the pot and brown them evenly, 8 to 10 minutes, turning every minute. Remove the breasts and set aside. Add the onion, carrots, leek, celery, garlic, clove, fennel seeds, thyme, bay leaves, and tarragon to the pot and cook for 5 minutes, stirring frequently.

2   Reduce the heat to low and cover. Cook for another 5 minutes. Uncover the pot, add the sherry, and cook for 3 minutes. Add 1 cup Champagne and bring to a simmer. Add the broth and heat until it's barely simmering (or as I say, smiling). Keep it barely simmering for 15 minutes. Then add the breasts back to the pot and cook for 7 more minutes.

3   Remove the breasts and legs and place on a platter. Cover with plastic wrap and let cool completely. Let the remaining liquid simmer for another 45 minutes, then strain it through a fine-mesh sieve. Return the liquid to the pot and bring to a simmer again. Add the bok choy and cook for 8 minutes. Remove the bok choy from the cooking liquid and set aside.

(continued)

4 Turn the heat to medium-low, bringing the liquid to a high simmer, and reduce the cooking liquid by one-third, about 10 minutes. Meanwhile, carve the breast meat off the bone, leaving the skin intact. (Leave the drumstick and thigh meat on the bone.)

5 Preheat the oven to 400°F.

6 Season the breast meat and legs with salt and pepper. Heat a large skillet over medium-high heat for 2 minutes. Melt the remaining 3 tablespoons butter in the skillet. Add the legs and breast meat, skin side down, to the skillet. Cook for 2 minutes. Add the bok choy to the skillet, and transfer the skillet to the oven. Roast for 8 minutes.

7 Divide the hen and bok choy evenly among 6 bowls. Bring the sauce in the skillet back to a simmer over medium-low heat and add the remaining ½ cup Champagne. Return it to a simmer, and then ladle it over the hen and bok choy. Serve immediately.

HOW TO CUT UP A GUINEA HEN

First, detach the legs at the joint between the drumstick and thigh with a boning knife or any sharp, heavy knife. Then, use kitchen shears to detach the back from the breast by cutting alongside the bottom part of each side of the breast—the back should drop out. Cut the back in half—this is used to add flavor to the dish, but you will not be serving it.

Pain Perdu with Roasted Pears and Honey-Thyme Apricots

This is a showstopper of a dessert. It's very festive, and it's actually really easy to make! Prepare the crème anglaise first, then make the apricots and let them sit and absorb the flavors while you prepare the pears and bread. The crème anglaise and apricots will keep at room temperature for 2 to 3 hours, or you can make them a day ahead and refrigerate them overnight. The Moscato paired with this dessert accentuates the flavors of the roasted pears and the apricots.

6 slices brioche, about ¾ inch thick

1 recipe Crème Anglaise (page 20)

2 tablespoons butter

1 Soak the brioche in the crème anglaise for 2 minutes or slightly less.

2 Place a large sauté pan over medium-high heat. Add the butter to the pan and heat until sizzling, about 1 minute. Add the brioche slices 3 at a time to the pan, and sear the slices for 2 to 3 minutes on each side, until golden brown. Keep the first batch warm in the oven. If you've just roasted the pears, the residual heat from the shut-off oven should suffice; if not, turn the oven to 200°F.

3 Serve with the Honey-Thyme Apricots (page 20) spooned over the top and the Roasted Pears (page 21) alongside.

Crème Anglaise

2 cups milk

⅓ cup sugar

1 vanilla bean

5 large egg yolks

1 Prepare an ice bath (facing page).

2 Combine the milk, sugar, and vanilla bean in a medium-size saucepan. Bring the mixture to a boil over medium-high heat.

3 Reduce the heat to low. Place the egg yolks in a medium-size bowl and whisk about ½ cup of the hot milk mixture into the yolks to temper them. When well incorporated, pour the yolk mixture back into the saucepan and stir the mixture constantly with a wooden spoon until it's thick enough to coat a spoon, about 5 minutes (or until it has reached about 160°F on an instant-read thermometer). Strain the mixture through a fine-mesh sieve into the bowl in the ice bath and stir until it's cooled.

Honey-Thyme Apricots

1 cup dried apricots

2 tablespoons water

¼ cup sherry

1 tablespoon honey

1 teaspoon pure vanilla extract

3 sprigs fresh thyme

Combine the apricots, water, sherry, honey, vanilla, and thyme in a medium-size saucepan and bring to a simmer over medium heat. Simmer for 2 minutes, then remove from the heat. Cover and let stand for 1 hour before serving.

Roasted Pears

3 tablespoons butter

3 Anjou pears, split lengthwise and cored

2 tablespoons sugar

1 vanilla bean, split lengthwise and scraped

3 tablespoons brandy

Pinch of salt and cracked black pepper

1 Preheat the oven to 350°F.

2 Melt the butter in a medium-size sauté pan over medium heat. When the butter begins to smoke (this should take about 4 minutes), place the pears flesh side down in the pan and cook for about 4 minutes, or until brown.

3 Turn the pears and cook them on the other side for 3 minutes. Remove the pan from the heat. Remove the pears from the pan and set aside.

4 Add the sugar to the pan and blend with the residual butter. Add the vanilla bean pod and scrapings and the brandy. Return the pan to the burner over medium heat and cook off some of the alcohol, about 1 minute. Remove from the heat, toss the pears with the liquid, and sprinkle the salt and pepper over the pears. Place them in a roasting pan flesh side down.

5 Roast the pears in the oven for 3 to 5 minutes. Remove from the oven and baste them with the juices from the roasting pan. Serve warm, at room temperature, or chilled.

PREPARING AN ICE BATH
Fill a large bowl halfway with water and ice, then nestle a smaller bowl in the ice water that's in the larger bowl. Be careful to ensure that none of the ice water drips into the smaller bowl.

BORDEAUX

Bordeaux is the most popular theme of all of our Wine Mondays. It's French, of course, which many people think of as the epitome of wine. And Bordeaux is the most famous wine region of all, loaded with history and famous names (think Château Mouton-Rothschild, Château Lafite-Rothschild, and Château Margaux). The grape varietals are familiar, too—mainly Cabernet Sauvignon, Merlot, and Cabernet Franc—and it's easy to find decent, well-priced wines from

Bordeaux in most wine stores. (Plus, if you're willing to pay for it, you can actually go into a store and buy something like a Château Latour—whereas it can be impossible to find the legendary wines from Burgundy.) Red Bordeaux tends to be big and tannic and great with red meat; there are also great white Bordeaux wines, made from Sauvignon Blanc, Sémillon, and Muscadelle grapes, plus sweet Sauternes.

WINTER → **Bordeaux**

MENU

& pairings

↓

 +

PAIRINGS

1

Sautéed Shrimp with Brown Sugar, Chili-Glazed Pink Grapefruit, and Citrus Hollandaise

2005 Château Thieuley, Blanc, Bordeaux

2

Grilled Quail with Wild Rice, Pomegranate, and Watercress Salad

2001 Château Villa Bel-Air, Graves

3

Standing Rib Roast with Ruby Mustard, Roasted Eggplant, and Peas with Mint and Garlic

2000 S De Siran, Margaux

4

Lavender Crème Brûlée

2003 Château La Fleur d'Or, Sauternes

WINE NOTES

↓

1ST PAIRING **SAUTÉED SHRIMP WITH BROWN SUGAR,**
CHILI-GLAZED PINK GRAPEFRUIT, AND CITRUS HOLLANDAISE
SERVED WITH → **2005 CHÂTEAU THIEULEY, BLANC, BORDEAUX**

The fruitiness of white Bordeaux works well with the citrus and hint of spice in this dish, which would also be delicious accompanied by almost any rich, full-bodied Sauvignon Blanc.

2ND PAIRING **GRILLED QUAIL WITH WILD RICE, POMEGRANATE, AND WATERCRESS SALAD**
SERVED WITH → **2001 CHÂTEAU VILLA BEL-AIR, GRAVES**

Graves wines are always aromatic, generally with some violet, lavender, and mineral notes. They aren't especially tough or tannic, but they're still big—and that's the kind of wine that works well with this dish: flavorful, but nothing too overpowering, so that the subtle flavors of the quail and wild rice can come through.

3RD PAIRING **STANDING RIB ROAST WITH RUBY MUSTARD,**
ROASTED EGGPLANT, AND PEAS WITH MINT AND GARLIC
SERVED WITH → **2000 S DE SIRAN, MARGAUX**

Margaux is a soft, lighter-style Bordeaux, without the tannins of other Bordeaux wines. If you can't find a Margaux, you could try a light Cabernet-based wine—maybe something from Washington State.

4TH PAIRING **LAVENDER CRÈME BRÛLÉE**
SERVED WITH → **2003 CHÂTEAU LA FLEUR D'OR, SAUTERNES**

We pair this dessert with a Sauternes from Château La Fleur d'Or. A Sauternes wine is generally very sweet and rich, with notes of honey, flowers, and raisin. But they tend to be balanced, not sickly sweet, thanks to enough acidity to play against the sugar. A good alternative would be another Sauternes or an Italian Moscato.

Sautéed Shrimp with
Brown Sugar, Chili-Glazed Pink Grapefruit,
and Citrus Hollandaise

Shrimp is one of my favorite ways to start any menu. It's sexy, sweet, and not too rich. Here it plays against citrus and a hint of spice. If you would like to add greens to this composition, try a small amount of baby spinach salad.

2 pink grapefruits

2 tablespoons canola oil

1 shallot, minced

2 garlic cloves, minced

2 teaspoons chili powder

¼ teaspoon curry powder

¼ teaspoon ground coriander

¼ teaspoon whole fennel seeds

Pinch of crushed red pepper

1 tablespoon plus 1 teaspoon
    brown sugar

1 tablespoon brandy

1 tablespoon white wine

Zest of 1 orange (preferably a
    blood orange, if in season)

Zest of 1 lime

½ teaspoon salt

18 large shrimp, peeled and
    deveined

3 scallions

1 tablespoon cold butter

1 Section the grapefruits (facing page) and reserve ¼ cup of the juice for the shrimp marinade and ¼ cup of the juice to make the Citrus Hollandaise (page 28). Set aside the grapefruit sections in a large bowl.

2 To make the shrimp marinade, heat a small nonreactive sauté pan over medium-high heat for 2 minutes. Add 1 tablespoon of the canola oil and the shallot. Stir with a wooden spoon for 30 seconds, then add the garlic. Add the chili powder, curry powder, coriander, fennel seeds, crushed red pepper, and brown sugar and reduce the heat to low. Cook for 1½ minutes, stirring constantly, making sure not to let it burn. Add the brandy, then the wine, and cook for 15 seconds before adding ¼ cup reserved grapefruit juice and the citrus zests. Bring to a simmer and cook for 2 minutes over very low heat. Remove from the heat, pour into a bowl, season with salt, and set aside to cool.

3 Combine the shrimp with the marinade and toss gently to coat. Refrigerate, covered, for 1 to 4 hours.

4 Cut the scallions into ¼-inch-thick slices. Add to the bowl with the grapefruit sections.

5 Heat a large sauté pan over high heat for 2½ minutes. Add the remaining 1 tablespoon canola oil and completely coat the sauté pan. Add the butter. When the butter is sizzling and popping, evenly distribute the shrimp across the surface of the pan and reduce the heat to medium-high. Cook for 3 to 4 minutes, tossing and stirring at the same time, or until the shrimp have lost their translucence. Pour any residual marinade over the shrimp and heat thoroughly. Remove from the heat and toss with the grapefruit sections and scallions.

6 To serve, ladle one large dollop of Citrus Hollandaise (page 28) onto each of 6 warm plates. Spoon the shrimp mixture over the edges of the hollandaise sauce.

CITRUS FRUIT PREPARATION

Here's how to prepare a grapefruit (or any citrus fruit) if you want both beautiful sections that look fantastic in a dish and as much juice as you can squeeze.

1 Using a sharp chef's knife, slice the ends off the grapefruit so that the flesh is just exposed.

2 Place the grapefruit flat side down and use the knife to carve off the rind, rotating the grapefruit until it is completely peeled.

3 Use the knife to slice out sections between the membranes—the meat of the section should fall out easily. Continue around the grapefruit until all the wedges are detached from the membrane. Set the sections aside.

4 The remaining membrane should be very juicy—squeeze it thoroughly through a strainer and reserve the juice.

Citrus Hollandaise

I use olive oil, not just butter, in this hollandaise to give it more structure and a hint of the fruity taste of olives.

1 tablespoon canola oil

1 shallot, minced

¼ cup fresh pink grapefruit juice

Juice of 1 orange (blood orange, if possible)

Juice of 1 lime

1 tablespoon dried tarragon, or 2 tablespoons minced fresh tarragon

¼ teaspoon freshly ground white pepper

3 large egg yolks

½ teaspoon salt

½ garlic clove, minced

Pinch of cayenne pepper

2 dashes of Worcestershire sauce

½ cup (1 stick) butter, melted

6 tablespoons extra virgin olive oil

1 Heat a medium-size saucepan over medium-high heat for 2 minutes. Add the canola oil and heat for 30 seconds. Add the shallot and stir for 15 seconds. Stir in the citrus juices, tarragon, if dried (if fresh, reserve), and white pepper. Reduce the liquid by half, which should take 3 to 4 minutes. Strain into a medium-size bowl and whisk in the egg yolks, keeping the mixture warm by whisking over a pot of simmering water or in a double boiler over low heat.

2 Fill a 4-quart saucepan with ½ inch of water and place over low heat. Place the bowl with the egg mixture over the pot. Add the salt, garlic, cayenne, and Worcestershire sauce to the mixture and whisk for 2 minutes. Pour in the butter in a steady stream, whisking slowly and constantly to emulsify. Stop pouring in the butter periodically (but keep whisking!) to ensure proper emulsification. Add the fresh tarragon, if using. When the butter is fully emulsified, add the olive oil, following the same process used to emulsify the butter. Taste for seasoning and set the sauce aside in a warm place until ready to serve. (If you keep it on a burner, make sure the heat is *very* low.)

Grilled Quail with Wild Rice, Pomegranate, and Watercress Salad

Lately it seems that everyone wants quail when they see it on a menu. And with good reason: Quail is a wonderful example of a game bird, combining richness with delicate sweetness. In this dish, the texture of the wild rice and the tang of pomegranate in the salad helps the quail's flavor come through. You can find boneless quail in many butcher shops.

¼ cup pomegranate juice

1 shallot, chopped

1 teaspoon Dijon mustard

1 garlic clove

3 juniper berries

½ teaspoon dried thyme

1 tablespoon red wine

1 tablespoon canola oil

¼ teaspoon freshly ground black pepper, plus more for seasoning

¼ teaspoon ground allspice

6 boneless quails, rinsed and patted dry

Salt

1 Combine the pomegranate juice, shallot, mustard, garlic, juniper berries, thyme, red wine, canola oil, pepper, and allspice in a blender and blend for 1 minute. Pour into a nonreactive baking dish, add the quails, and toss gently to coat. Cover and marinate in the refrigerator for at least 1 hour and up to overnight.

2 Prepare a hot fire in a charcoal grill, or preheat your gas grill (or a grill pan) to high. Season each quail on both sides with salt and pepper. Evenly distribute the quails on the grill surface and cover. After 2 minutes, remove the cover and rotate the quails 90 degrees, keeping them on the same side. Re-cover and cook for 2 minutes. Flip the quails and repeat the grilling process on the other side for an additional 4 minutes. At this point, the quail should be pink inside and done (about 155°F on an instant-read thermometer).

3 Prepare the Wild Rice, Pomegranate, and Watercress Salad (page 30). Spoon the wild rice onto the center of a serving platter. Place the quails side by side on top of the rice and distribute the dressed watercress evenly along the edges of the platter on both sides of the rice.

Wild Rice, Pomegranate, and Watercress Salad

1 cup long-grain wild rice

2 tablespoons butter

1 tablespoon canola oil

1 medium-size onion, diced

2 celery stalks, peeled and diced

1 medium-size carrot, peeled
and diced

2 garlic cloves, minced

1 teaspoon dried *herbes de
Provence* (facing page)

1½ cups vegetable broth, plus
more if needed

1 teaspoon salt

Seeds of 1 pomegranate
(about 1 cup; page 170)

Pomegranate Vinaigrette (recipe
follows)

1 bunch watercress, 1 inch of the
stems trimmed

1 Preheat the oven to 350°F.

2 Bring 2 quarts of salted water to a boil in a
4-quart saucepan. Add the wild rice to the
boiling water and cook for 6 minutes, then
drain.

3 Place an ovenproof 3-quart pot over
medium-high heat, and add the butter
and canola oil. When the butter is slightly
browned (this should take about 2 minutes),
add the onion and stir with a wooden spoon
for 1 to 2 minutes, or until the onion is
translucent. Add the celery, carrot, garlic,
and *herbes de Provence*, and cook for 2
minutes. Add the cooked wild rice to the
vegetables and stir. Stir in the vegetable
broth and cover. Bring to a simmer.

4 Cover the pot, transfer to the oven, and
cook for 45 minutes, or until the rice grains
begin to pop. Add more broth if needed.
Cook until the rice is still chewy, but not
mushy.

5 Pour off any extra liquid and add 1 tablespoon of the liquid to the vinaigrette, if
possible. Place the rice in a large bowl,
season with salt, add the pomegranate seeds
and three-quarters of the vinaigrette, and
toss. Toss the remaining vinaigrette with the
watercress in a separate bowl.

Pomegranate Vinaigrette

4 tablespoons pomegranate juice

1 tablespoon fresh lime juice

2 teaspoons red wine vinegar

1 teaspoon soy sauce

1 teaspoon Dijon mustard

½ garlic clove, minced

¼ teaspoon ground thyme

2 tablespoons walnut oil

2 tablespoons olive oil

In a small bowl, combine the pomegranate and lime juices, vinegar, soy sauce, mustard, garlic, and thyme. Add the oils and whisk to blend.

HERBES DE PROVENCE

As the name suggests, this is a mix of herbs that originated in Provence—and the flavors are associated with Provençal cooking. Prepared Provençal herb mixes generally contain sage, thyme, rosemary, oregano, and sometimes lavender. Thyme is often the dominant flavor in the mix.

Standing Rib Roast with
Ruby Mustard, Roasted Eggplant, and
Peas with Mint and Garlic

A beautiful standing rib roast feels like the perfect holiday or winter celebration meal to me. It's special and delicious, but also warm and comforting—and ideal with a sturdy, rich Margaux. One of the few vegetables I'll buy frozen are peas. Use organic baby peas if you can.

3 tablespoons coarse sea salt

2 teaspoons freshly ground black pepper

6 garlic cloves, 3 peeled and 3 unpeeled

2 teaspoons dried thyme

1 teaspoon paprika

One 6-pound rib roast (3 ribs)

1 medium-size onion, peeled and chopped

2 carrots, peeled and chopped

3 celery stalks, peeled and chopped

1 leek, washed (page 195) and chopped into 1-inch sections

1 cup Madeira

1 cup chicken broth

1 Combine the salt, pepper, peeled garlic cloves, 1 teaspoon of the thyme, and the paprika in a mortar and mash with a pestle (if you don't have a mortar and pestle, mince the garlic and mash the ingredients together). Rub this mixture evenly over the entire rib roast, place the meat in a roasting pan, and let stand in a cool place for 1 to 3 hours before placing the roast in the oven. (Don't let the roast stand in the refrigerator —you want the meat at room temperature when you put it in the oven so that it will cook evenly.)

2 At least 20 minutes in advance of roasting, preheat the oven to 500°F.

3 Combine the onion, carrots, celery, and leek in a mixing bowl. Add the 3 unpeeled garlic cloves and the remaining 1 teaspoon thyme and mix together. Add the vegetable mixture to the roasting pan, surrounding the meat. Roast for 20 minutes, then turn the oven down to 300°F and stir the vegetables with a wooden spoon. Continue to roast for about

2 more hours. Pour the Madeira over the vegetables and roast for another 5 minutes. Add the chicken broth and roast for an additional 20 minutes. This should bring the internal temperature of the meat to 125°F, for rare. Another 14 minutes in the oven will give you medium-rare (and you can serve the outside slices to guests who prefer medium).

4   When the roast reaches the desired internal temperature, remove it from the oven and lift it onto a serving platter. Let the roast stand for 20 to 30 minutes before carving. Meanwhile, strain the liquid from the vegetables into a saucepan (you should have approximately ½ cup); discard the vegetables. Bring the sauce to a simmer for 3 minutes, and season with salt and pepper. Spoon the sauce over the sliced roast and serve with the Ruby Mustard, Roasted Eggplant, and Peas with Mint and Garlic (recipes follow).

Ruby Mustard

2 cups red wine

1 cup port

2 shallots, finely chopped

3 sprigs fresh thyme

½ cup Dijon mustard

1 tablespoon honey

½ teaspoon salt

½ teaspoon freshly ground black pepper

1   Combine the wine, port, shallots, and thyme in a large saucepan. Cook over medium heat for about 12 minutes, until the mixture is reduced to ½ cup of syrup.

2   Combine the mustard and honey in a small bowl. Pour the wine syrup through a fine-mesh sieve into the mustard-honey mixture and blend thoroughly. Add salt and pepper.

Roasted Eggplant

3 medium-size eggplants, sliced in half lengthwise

1 tablespoon salt

3 garlic cloves, minced

½ teaspoon dried basil

½ teaspoon dried oregano

½ teaspoon freshly ground black pepper

¼ cup olive oil

2 tablespoons balsamic vinegar

½ teaspoon Worcestershire sauce

3 tablespoons freshly grated Parmesan cheese

1 Arrange the eggplants skin side down on a sheet pan. Slice and score the flesh of each section. Evenly sprinkle the salt over the cut portions of the eggplant. Let stand for 30 to 45 minutes at room temperature.

2 Preheat the oven to 400°F.

3 Combine the garlic, basil, oregano, pepper, olive oil, vinegar, and Worcestershire sauce in a small bowl and evenly distribute over the cut portions of the eggplant. Let stand for 5 minutes. Roast for 30 minutes, or until golden brown. Remove from the oven and evenly distribute the cheese over the top of the eggplant. Bake for 7 more minutes.

Peas with Mint and Garlic

2 tablespoons extra virgin olive oil

¼ cup (½ stick) butter

½ of a medium-size onion, minced

1 garlic clove, minced

2 cups frozen peas, thawed

¼ cup minced fresh mint

Zest and juice of 1 lime

Salt and freshly ground black pepper

1 Heat the olive oil and butter in a medium-size saucepan over medium-high heat for about 2 minutes. Add the onion and stir with a wooden spoon for 4 minutes, or until translucent. Add the garlic and stir for 20 seconds, then stir in the peas. Reduce the heat to medium and cover. Cook for 6 minutes, uncovering to stir every 2 minutes.

2 Just before serving, stir in the mint, lime zest, and lime juice. Season with salt and pepper. Serve immediately.

Lavender Crème Brûlée

Crème brûlée was my favorite childhood dessert. My grandmother used to make it with goose eggs. This recipe calls for regular chicken eggs—use fresh, local, organic eggs if you can. The lavender flavor in this crème brûlée goes beautifully with Sauternes.

3½ cups heavy cream

1 cup whole milk

1 vanilla bean, split lengthwise

1½ tablespoons dried lavender

10 large egg yolks

1⅓ cups sugar

1 Preheat the oven to 325°F.

2 Combine the cream, milk, vanilla bean, and lavender in a heavy saucepan and bring to a boil. Remove from the heat and let stand for 20 minutes. Strain through a fine-mesh sieve into a bowl.

3 Place the egg yolks in a large mixing bowl. Beat with an electric mixer on medium speed, and slowly add ½ cup plus 1 tablespoon of the sugar to the egg yolks. Beat for 3 to 4 minutes, until completely smooth and opaque in color. Turn the mixer speed to low and continue to beat while adding 1 cup of the warm lavender cream. Once it's completely incorporated, add the remainder of the lavender cream and beat until well combined.

(continued)

4 Place six 8-ounce ramekins in a baking pan filled with enough water to reach halfway up the outside of the ramekins. Divide the crème brûlée mixture evenly among the ramekins. Cover the baking pan with aluminum foil. Place it in the oven and reduce the heat to 300°F. Bake for 45 minutes. To check for doneness, uncover and shake the baking pan gently to see if the custards are set. If they have not completely set, bake for an additional 5 minutes and try again. Let cool on a wire rack (or refrigerate overnight).

5 Just before you're ready to serve, distribute the remaining sugar evenly over the tops of the custards, creating a thin coating over the surfaces. With a kitchen torch or under a broiler, caramelize the sugar over the custard (about 1 minute, until the surface is golden brown). Serve immediately.

PLAYING WITH FLAVOR

You can create an entirely different taste experience by replacing the lavender in this crème brûlée recipe with fresh ginger, lemongrass, mint, or basil. Infuse the custard with the ingredient of your choice and proceed with the rest of the recipe.

BURGUNDY

If Bordeaux is one of the classic wine-producing regions in France, Burgundy is the other. And our Burgundy Wine Mondays are nearly as popular as our Bordeaux events. After Pinot Noir wine became hugely popular, people figured out that the Burgundy region is where most Pinot Noir grapes grow. Suddenly no one can get enough of Burgundy. The region is like a special patchwork quilt of Chardonnay and Pinot Noir vineyards—wines made from grapes growing in vineyards right next door to each other can taste completely different because there are so many different soil types. And because Pinot Noir is so subtle and transparent, it tends to take on the flavors of whatever went on during its growing season. The variations between wines, even from the same producer, can be palpable—but good Pinot Noir is fantastic with many kinds of food, especially salmon and chicken.

WINER → **Burgundy**

MENU

& pairings

↓

 +

PAIRINGS

Black Walnut, Granny Smith, and Chèvre Tarte Tatin	**1**	**Louis Bouillot, "Grande Réserve," Brut, Crémant de Bourgogne**
Pan-Roasted Black Bass with Shrimp Flan and Stir-Fried Shiitakes	**2**	**2004 Jean-Marc Brocard, Sauvignon de Saint-Bris**
Whole Roasted Tarragon Chicken with Roasted Chantenay Carrots	**3**	**2001 Domaine Carré-Courbin, "Les Lurets," Volnay Premier Cru**
Chocolate-Orange Soufflés with Chocolate-Espresso Crème Anglaise	**4**	**2001 Domaine Alain Burguet, "Les Pince Vin," Bourgogne**

WINE 📖 NOTES

↓

1ST PAIRING **BLACK WALNUT, GRANNY SMITH, AND CHÈVRE TARTE TATIN**
SERVED WITH → **LOUIS BOUILLOT, "GRANDE RÉSERVE," BRUT, CRÉMANT DE BOURGOGNE**

This is one of our favorite sparkling wines—it's part of the first course of our Bubbles, Bubbles Everywhere dinner (page 11). It's very similar to a Champagne (same grapes, same method), and it has notes of pear and apple that work well with goat cheese, especially when it's rich and melted as in this tarte tatin. A dry prosecco would also be great with this dish.

2ND PAIRING **PAN-ROASTED BLACK BASS WITH SHRIMP FLAN AND STIR-FRIED SHIITAKES**
SERVED WITH → **2004 JEAN-MARC BROCARD, SAUVIGNON DE SAINT-BRIS, BURGUNDY**

This is a fun wine, and an anomaly coming from Burgundy, because normally white Burgundy wines are Chardonnay. This is one of the few exceptions. There's a very small area in Burgundy where Sauvignon Blanc is grown, up to the north, close to Chablis. This wine features many of the same minerals you'd find in Chablis. Another Sauvignon Blanc aged in stainless steel would be good here—you just don't want something oaky, because that would interfere with the flavor of the bass.

3RD PAIRING **WHOLE ROASTED TARRAGON CHICKEN WITH ROASTED CHANTENAY CARROTS**
SERVED WITH → **2001 DOMAINE CARRÉ-COURBIN, "LES LURETS," VOLNAY PREMIER CRU**

This wine is a Pinot Noir, and L'Espalier wine director Erik Johnson's favorite thing to do is pair a simple roast chicken with a Pinot from Burgundy. This particular wine perfectly complements the tarragon chicken, because there are hints of tarragon flavor to the wine as well. Another earthy, soft Pinot from Burgundy would taste wonderful with this dish, too.

4TH PAIRING **CHOCOLATE-ORANGE SOUFFLÉS WITH CHOCOLATE-ESPRESSO CRÈME ANGLAISE**
SERVED WITH → **2001 DOMAINE ALAIN BURGUET, "LES PINCE VIN," BOURGOGNE**

The fruit for this wine comes from the Gevrey-Chambertin region in the north of Burgundy, and it's a fuller-style red Burgundy with nicely balanced flavor that pairs well with chocolate as long as the chocolate isn't too sweet (which this soufflé is not). Generally speaking, super-sugary desserts are not good with wine.

Black Walnut, Granny Smith, and Chèvre Tarte Tatin

We created this dish to pair with Champagne or sparkling wine. Many Champagnes and sparkling wines have a green apple flavor, so I wanted to use Granny Smiths in this tart. The nuttiness of the walnuts works well with the nuttiness of a brut Champagne, and goat cheese also tastes really good with Champagne. Look for black walnuts in specialty stores or better supermarkets, or substitute regular walnuts. Baking lore has it that the tarte tatin, an upside-down tart with caramelized apples, was first created in France by a lustful maiden who ran after a prince and left her apples cooking in butter and sugar until they caramelized—and she salvaged them in a tarte tatin. I like making a double recipe of Pâte Real, the pastry dough in this tart, and freezing the unused portion to have on hand anytime I want to make a pie or tart. Pâte Real is a rich dough that is sometimes called a quick puff pastry dough, because it has a little bounce to it. It's one of my favorite pastry crusts.

7 Granny Smith apples, peeled, cored, and cut into sixths

1 teaspoon minced fresh rosemary, or ½ teaspoon ground dried rosemary

1 teaspoon fresh lemon juice

3 tablespoons butter

3 tablespoons sugar

1 teaspoon salt

½ cup toasted black walnuts (page 171)

4 ounces soft (not aged) goat cheese

Pâte Real (page 42)

1 large egg

1 tablespoon milk

1   Preheat the oven to 400°F.

2   Place the apple pieces in a bowl. Add the rosemary and lemon juice and toss. Place a 10-inch nonreactive, ovenproof skillet or tatin pan over medium-high heat. Add the butter. When the butter is completely melted, add the sugar and salt, stirring with a wooden spoon until it bubbles and a slight caramel color develops. Arrange half of the apples in a fan pattern in the butter mixture (this will be the top of your tatin), and evenly distribute half of the walnuts over the apples. Combine the remaining apples and walnuts in a bowl and distribute evenly on top of the walnuts in the pan. Dot the apple and walnut layer with the goat cheese, distributing it as evenly as possible.

(continued)

3 Remove the skillet from the heat. Drape the Pâte Real dough over the apples, tucking any overhanging dough down between the apples and the inside edge of the skillet. Beat the egg with the milk, and brush the dough with the egg-milk mixture. Place the skillet in the oven and reduce the heat to 375°F. Bake for 30 minutes, or until the pastry is golden. Remove and let cool on a wire rack for 15 minutes.

4 Loosen the edges of the pastry with a knife. Quickly and carefully invert the tarte tatin onto a platter and serve.

Pâte Real

1 cup all-purpose flour

½ teaspoon salt

1 cup (2 sticks) butter

1 tablespoon plus 2 teaspoons
  heavy cream

2 large egg yolks

½ teaspoon fresh lemon juice

1 Place the flour and salt in a food processor and pulse to blend. Add the butter and pulse until the mixture looks like fine meal. Dump the mixture onto a floured work surface and form a well in the center. Place the cream, egg yolks, and lemon juice into the well. Knead together, incorporating the meal into the wet ingredients until the dough holds its shape, about 3 to 4 minutes, making sure not to overknead.

2 Place the dough on a floured surface. Roll into a 12-inch circle, about ¼ inch thick. Place on a flat sheet pan and refrigerate, covered with plastic wrap, for at least 20 minutes and up to overnight. (This also keeps well in the freezer for up to 1 month.)

GOING ALL OUT

If you want to really go over the top with your tarte tatin, make this glaze, which adds a zesty component with tons of flavor, and finish with this prosciutto topping. The glaze is also fantastic in a ham sandwich.

Spiced Citrus Mustard Glaze

1 cup sugar

1 cup white wine

2 cups fresh orange juice

½ cup champagne vinegar or white wine vinegar

1 tablespoon chili powder

1 teaspoon cayenne pepper

1 tablespoon Dijon mustard

1 Combine the sugar and a splash of water in a medium-size saucepan over medium-high heat and cook, stirring to moisten the sugar, until the sugar develops a caramel color, about 5 minutes (watch it closely to make sure it doesn't burn).

2 Add the white wine, orange juice, and vinegar to the sugar and reduce the liquid by half (this should take about 10 minutes). Reduce by half again, about another 5 minutes. Stir in the chili powder and cayenne, then fold in the mustard. Remove from the heat and let cool. Spoon the sauce onto each of 6 plates before placing a section of tarte tatin on top.

Crispy Prosciutto

6 large, thin slices prosciutto

1 Preheat the oven to 350°F.

2 Place the prosciutto on a sheet pan, evenly spaced, and bake for 12 minutes, or until crispy. Remove, let cool, and lean a crispy piece against each slice of tarte tatin.

Pan-Roasted Black Bass with Shrimp Flan and Stir-Fried Shiitakes

This preparation works with any type of bass. Bass fillets are known for their sweetness and tenderness and ability to pick up other flavors. Here I've chosen aromatic Asian-inspired flavors that play off the nuances of the bass. If you're serving the flan with the bass, you can make the flan in advance and let it sit at room temperature for 45 minutes before serving.

3 tablespoons fresh grapefruit juice

1 tablespoon fresh lime juice

1 tablespoon light soy sauce

1 garlic clove, minced

½ teaspoon crushed red pepper

1 stalk lemongrass, pounded and chopped

1 tablespoon grated fresh ginger

8 scallions, thinly sliced on the bias

1 tablespoon brown sugar

1 teaspoon red curry paste

4 tablespoons canola oil

Six 4-ounce black bass fillets

1 tablespoon coarse sea salt

1 teaspoon freshly ground white pepper

4 tablespoons chopped fresh basil

1 Combine the grapefruit and lime juices with the soy sauce, garlic, crushed red pepper, lemongrass, ginger, scallions, brown sugar, curry paste, and 1 tablespoon of the canola oil in a medium-size bowl.

2 Place the bass fillets in a large, shallow dish, skin side up. Pour the marinade over the fish, distributing it evenly over the fillets. Refrigerate for 1 hour.

3 Preheat the oven to 400°F.

4 Remove the fillets from the marinade and set the marinade aside. Season the flesh side of the fillets with the salt and pepper. Heat a medium-size ovenproof sauté pan over high heat for 3 minutes. Reduce the heat to medium-high and add the remaining 3 tablespoons canola oil. Heat the oil for 1 minute, then place the fillets in the pan, skin side down. Moving quickly, retrieve the scallions from the marinade and add about half of them to the pan. (Discard the remaining scallions, but reserve the marinade.) After the bass has been in the pan for about 2 minutes, remove the pan from the burner, place it on the middle rack of the oven, and bake for 4 minutes.

5 Pour the marinade into a small saucepan and reduce the liquid by half, about 4 minutes. Set aside.

6 Remove the pan from the oven and let it sit for 2 to 4 minutes on a cool burner. Lift the fillets out of the pan with an offset spatula and place them on a serving platter. Spoon the reduced marinade over them. Sprinkle with the basil and serve with Shrimp Flan (page 46) and Stir-Fried Shiitakes (recipe follows).

Stir-Fried Shiitakes

¼ pound (about 2 cups) shiitake mushrooms

2 tablespoons peanut oil

1 shallot, minced

1 garlic clove, minced

1 tablespoon light soy sauce

1 teaspoon salt

½ teaspoon freshly ground black pepper

1 Slice the mushrooms about ¼ inch thick. Place a wok or medium-size sauté pan over high heat for 3 minutes. Add the oil and heat for 30 seconds, evenly distributing the oil over the wok. Be sure not to let the oil burn. Add the shallot and garlic and cook for 10 seconds. Add the mushrooms and stir so that they all make contact with the surface of the wok.

2 Add the soy sauce, salt, and pepper and mix well. Cover, reduce the heat to low, and cook for 3 minutes. Serve immediately.

ROASTING BASS

For every 1 inch of thickness, roast bass for 8 to 10 minutes (so you'd roast a ½-inch-thick fillet for 4 to 5 minutes) at 400°F. This will cook the fish to medium. For medium-rare, reduce the cooking time by about 10 percent.

Shrimp Flan

½ pound shrimp, peeled and deveined

1 garlic clove, minced

1 teaspoon pickled ginger

Zest of ½ orange

Zest of 1 lime

1 teaspoon fresh lemon juice

½ teaspoon ginger juice

¼ cup chopped scallions (green parts only)

½ teaspoon cayenne pepper

¼ teaspoon ground nutmeg

3 tablespoons fresh cilantro, finely chopped, plus 6 whole leaves for garnish

2 teaspoons salt

1 large egg, separated, white lightly beaten

2 tablespoons butter, at room temperature

3 tablespoons olive oil

½ teaspoon freshly ground white pepper

4 tablespoons heavy cream

6 pimientos or small pieces of sweet red bell pepper

1 Place the shrimp in a medium-size bowl. Add the garlic, ginger, orange and lime zests, lemon and ginger juices, scallions, cayenne, nutmeg, chopped cilantro, and salt and stir to combine. Let stand for 15 to 30 minutes. Meanwhile, place a food processor bowl in the freezer.

2 Preheat the oven to 350°F.

3 Pour the shrimp mixture into the chilled food processor bowl and puree for 2 to 3 minutes, or until smooth, stopping a few times to scrape the sides of the bowl to ensure that all the ingredients are evenly pureed.

4 Slowly drizzle the lightly beaten egg white into the mixture with the food processor running. Add the yolk. When the yolk is incorporated, add the butter. When the butter is incorporated, add the olive oil and blend. Add the white pepper and cream and blend until incorporated.

5 Oil six 4-ounce ramekins. Evenly distribute the shrimp mixture among the ramekins. Garnish the top of each with a cilantro leaf and a pimiento before baking. Place the ramekins into a shallow *bain-marie* (also known as a water bath—fill a baking pan with enough water to come up about one-third of the way on the outsides of the ramekins). Cover the pan with aluminum foil and bake for 25 minutes, or until set. Remove from the oven and let stand on a wire rack for at least 10 minutes. Remove the foil and unmold the flans onto individual plates.

Whole Roasted Tarragon Chicken with Roasted Chantenay Carrots

Tarragon and chicken is a match made in heaven—a classic, tried-and-true, French-inspired combination. Tarragon has aromatic, lemony nuances that bring out the flavor in the chicken. I always like including a straightforward roast chicken on Burgundy-inspired menus, because Burgundy is known for producing the best chickens in the world. Chantenay carrots are the sweetest on the market. They are a French variety that are left in the ground until the ground freezes, which boosts their sugar content. You can usually find them in late fall and winter, but regular carrots work just fine, too.

One 3½-pound roaster chicken, preferably organic free-range

2 lemons

1 tablespoon dried tarragon

4 garlic cloves, crushed

1 teaspoon salt

2 garlic cloves, minced

1 shallot, sliced

2 teaspoons paprika

1 teaspoon freshly ground black pepper

1 tablespoon brown sugar

1 tablespoon canola oil

½ teaspoon Worcestershire sauce

1 tablespoon Dijon mustard

1 teaspoon ground coriander

1 cup water

1 Remove the giblets and neck from the chicken. Wash the neck and chicken thoroughly in your sink and pat dry; set aside, covered, in a cool place. If making the Chicken Liver Croutons (page 49), wash the liver and set aside. Discard the other giblets.

2 Juice the lemons and reserve the juice. Chop up the lemon rind and place it in a small bowl. Add the tarragon, crushed garlic, and the salt.

3 Stuff the cavity of the chicken with the lemon rind mixture and truss the legs together with butcher's twine (page 149). Combine the reserved lemon juice, minced garlic, shallot, paprika, pepper, brown sugar, canola oil, Worcestershire sauce, mustard, and coriander in a bowl large enough to accommodate the chicken and whisk until well combined. Reserve 1 tablespoon of the marinade if making croutons.

4 Holding the chicken by its legs, immerse it in the marinade. If you've reserved the liver to make the croutons, marinate it in a separate small bowl in the 1 tablespoon of reserved marinade. Cover the chicken and

(continued)

marinate in the refrigerator for 4 hours or overnight.

5 Preheat the oven to 425°F.

6 Place the chicken, breast side up, and the neck in a casserole dish. Pour the marinade over the top of the chicken; bake for 20 minutes. Turn the chicken so the breast side is down, add the water to the baking dish, and bake for an additional 20 minutes. Flip the chicken again, reduce the oven temperature to 350°F, and bake for another 20 minutes.

7 Remove the pan from the oven and lift the chicken out of the pan, letting the juices drain into the pan. Place the chicken on a cutting board, cover with aluminum foil, and let rest for 15 minutes.

8 Strain the juices from the pan through a fine-mesh sieve into a large saucepan. With a small ladle or spoon, skim any fat off the surface of the liquid and discard. Heat the liquid over medium heat and reduce by half, about 6 minutes. Season with salt and pepper to taste.

9 Carve the chicken breast and legs and place on a serving platter, spooning the sauce over the top.

Roasted Chantenay Carrots

6 large Chantenay or regular carrots, peeled and cut into 4-inch sticks

1 teaspoon dried tarragon

1 teaspoon salt

Zest of 1 orange

2 tablespoons peanut oil

1 Preheat the oven to 350°F.

2 Place the carrots in a medium-size bowl and toss with the tarragon, salt, and orange zest. Heat a medium-size cast-iron skillet over high heat for 2 minutes. Reduce the heat to medium and add the oil. Heat for 30 seconds, then add the carrots.

3 Cook for 3 minutes, stirring frequently. Place the skillet in the oven and roast for 15 to 20 minutes, or until the carrots are golden brown.

GOING ALL OUT

When I make a chicken I always do something with the chicken liver because it is loaded with flavor. These croutons add nice flavor and crunch to the chicken, and they also make delicious hors d'oeuvres on their own.

Chicken Liver Croutons

1 tablespoon canola oil

Marinated liver from
   1 chicken (reserved from
   Whole Roasted Tarragon
   Chicken, page 47)

1 shallot, thinly sliced

½ teaspoon salt

¼ teaspoon freshly ground
   black pepper

½ teaspoon dried tarragon

¼ teaspoon ground nutmeg

1 tablespoon butter

3 slices fig or sourdough
   bread, cut into quarters and
   toasted

1   Preheat a small saucepan over high heat for 3 minutes. Reduce the heat to medium-high and add the canola oil. Add the liver and shallot to the pan. Cook the liver for 1½ minutes on each side. Reduce the heat to medium. Add the salt, pepper, tarragon, and nutmeg and toss.

2   Remove the pan from the heat and let cool for 5 minutes. Pour the contents of the pan into a food processor and puree until smooth. Add the butter and puree to emulsify. Scrape the mixture out of the food processor and taste for seasoning. Spread the mixture onto the toast and serve.

Chocolate-Orange Soufflés with Chocolate-Espresso Crème Anglaise

Don't be intimidated by the idea of making a soufflé. Even standard soufflés are totally doable, but chocolate soufflés are the absolute easiest because the chocolate adds structure and makes them less likely to collapse. But you don't have to tell your guests that—let them be impressed.

4 tablespoons all-purpose flour

3 tablespoons unsweetened cocoa powder

½ cup chopped bittersweet chocolate

⅓ cup plus 1 tablespoon sugar

1 cup milk

1 teaspoon pure vanilla extract

12 large eggs, separated

2 tablespoons Grand Marnier

Zest of 1 orange

2 tablespoons butter

1 Combine the flour, cocoa powder, chopped chocolate, and 1 tablespoon sugar in a small bowl and whisk to combine. In a separate bowl, lightly whisk together the milk, vanilla extract, and 3 of the egg yolks. Pour this mixture into the dry ingredients and whisk until thoroughly incorporated.

2 Pour the mixture into a medium-size saucepan and heat on medium-high, stirring constantly until it begins to thicken, approximately 5 minutes. Reduce the heat to medium-low and stir for about 4 minutes, or until the mixture bubbles.

3 Transfer the mixture to a small bowl and press plastic wrap onto the surface to keep the pastry cream from developing a skin while cooling. Let cool for 1 to 2 hours.

4 Preheat the oven to 350°F.

5 Add 7 of the egg yolks and the Grand Marnier to the cooled pastry cream and whisk until fully incorporated. Combine the 12 egg whites in a large mixing bowl and beat with an electric mixer until frothed, about 4 minutes. Slowly add ⅓ cup sugar and beat until medium-stiff peaks form.

6 Fold one-third of the egg white mixture into the pastry cream. Gently fold in the next third of the egg white mixture, being careful not to overmix. Gently fold in the last third of the egg white mixture, again being careful not to overmix. Gently fold in the orange zest.

7 Butter six 12-ounce ramekins. Divide the batter evenly among the ramekins and bake for 15 minutes. Serve immediately with Chocolate-Espresso Crème Anglaise (recipe follows). Puncture the top of the hot soufflés and pour the sauce right in.

Chocolate-Espresso Crème Anglaise

2 cups milk

⅓ cup sugar

3 tablespoons unsweetened cocoa powder

1 vanilla bean, split lengthwise and scraped

¼ cup unflavored ground coffee beans

5 large egg yolks

¾ cup chopped bittersweet chocolate

1 Prepare an ice bath (page 21).

2 Combine the milk, sugar, cocoa powder, vanilla bean pod and scrapings, and ground coffee in a medium-size saucepan. Bring to a boil over medium-high heat.

3 Reduce the heat to low. Place the egg yolks in a medium-size bowl and whisk about ½ cup of the hot liquid into the yolks to temper them. When well incorporated, pour the yolk mixture back into the pan and stir the mixture constantly with a wooden spoon until it's thick enough to coat a spoon, about 5 minutes (about 160°F on an instant-read thermometer).

4 Place the chopped chocolate into a bowl, pour the warm mixture over the chocolate, and whisk to emulsify. Strain the mixture through a fine-mesh sieve into the bowl in the ice bath and stir until it has cooled. Serve at room temperature.

RED IN THE FACE

Every so often we love doing an all-red tasting. Red wine drinkers are often passionately committed to drinking red and would prefer to skip the whites altogether. You can do that and still go from light to heavy wine—and find wines to pair with every course. The name of this Wine Monday was inspired by chefs' reputations for having tempers—and occasionally getting a little (or a lot) red in the face. But usually that anger is nothing some laughter and a good glass of red wine can't fix.

Whole Roasted Tarragon Chicken with Roasted Chantenay Carrots, PAGE 47

Sautéed Shrimp with Brown Sugar, Chili-Glazed
Pink Grapefruit, and Citrus Hollandaise, PAGE 26

Maine Lobster and Avocado Club Sandwich with Smoked Paprika Potato Chips, PAGE 88

Alaskan King Salmon with Black Quinoa and Cherries, PAGE 80

Walnut-Encrusted Spring Lamb with Bacon-Potato Rösti, PAGE 82

Standing Rib Roast with Ruby Mustard, Roasted Eggplant, and Peas with Mint and Garlic, PAGE 32

Pot-Roasted Pork with Chorizo and Clams, PAGE 73

Pot-au-Feu of Poussin with Spring Vegetables and Foie Gras, PAGE 102

WINTER → **Red in the Face**

MENU
& pairings
↓

  +

PAIRINGS

Seared Half-Cured Salmon with Aunt Midge's Sauce and Mustard Greens	**2003 Montinore Estate, Pinot Noir, Willamette Valley, Oregon**
Crispy Confit Duck Hash with Black Kale and Poached Eggs	**2001 Cave de Rasteau, "Prestige," Rasteau Côtes du Rhône-Villages, France**
Roasted Peppered Venison with Red Currant–Zinfandel Sauce and Celery Root and Parsnips	**2002 Mauritson, Zinfandel, Dry Creek Valley, California**
Ricotta Tarts with Pine Nuts and Cocoa Nibs	**Graham's, "Six Grapes," Oporto, Portugal**

WINE ⌷ NOTES

↓

1ST PAIRING **SEARED HALF-CURED SALMON WITH AUNT MIDGE'S SAUCE AND MUSTARD GREENS**
SERVED WITH → 2003 MONTINORE ESTATE, PINOT NOIR, WILLAMETTE VALLEY, OREGON

We start with a light wine for the first course and move through bolder, fuller wines as the dinner progresses. Pinot Noir has become exceedingly popular in recent years, and when it's good it's an ideal light red wine. However, if you find a Pinot you don't like, don't get discouraged. Pinot Noir is a fickle, thin-skinned grape that likes a cool climate (such as you find in Oregon) but can't get too wet, and it is more susceptible than others to rot. It really needs to be taken care of in the field, and it can't be easily blended with other varieties or treated with a lot of oak to mask problems with the fruit. So when you find one you love, enjoy it!

2ND PAIRING **CRISPY CONFIT DUCK HASH WITH BLACK KALE AND POACHED EGGS**
SERVED WITH → 2001 CAVE DE RASTEAU, "PRESTIGE," RASTEAU CÔTES DU RHÔNE-VILLAGES, FRANCE

Grenache is the predominant grape in this wine, which comes from a region in the Côtes du Rhône. It has flavors of cherry and black pepper that work really well with duck—the sweet, gamey earthiness plays well against Grenache.

3RD PAIRING **ROASTED PEPPERED VENISON WITH
RED CURRANT–ZINFANDEL SAUCE AND CELERY ROOT AND PARSNIPS**
SERVED WITH → 2002 MAURITSON, ZINFANDEL, DRY CREEK VALLEY, CALIFORNIA

Zinfandel and venison is one of our favorite combinations. Venison is lean, but it has a nice peppery, spicy flavor. The marinade for this venison has juniper berries, currants, rosemary, and thyme—and Zinfandel is beautiful with aromatic spices and fruit. Some Zinfandel is so rich, bold, and high in alcohol that it's difficult to pair with food—so look for one that's a little mellower, with a dense core and elegant fruity notes.

4TH PAIRING **RICOTTA TARTS WITH PINE NUTS AND COCOA NIBS**
SERVED WITH → GRAHAM'S, "SIX GRAPES," OPORTO, PORTUGAL

Port has a little bit of a chocolate essence to it and can also have a nice citrus flavor, so it goes well with a cheese-based dessert with hints of chocolate and orange. Another good pairing with this tart would be a dessert wine from the Greek island of Samos, where they make a mean Muscat. Samos has been famous for its dessert wine for more than 2,000 years.

Seared Half-Cured Salmon with
Aunt Midge's Sauce and Mustard Greens

We cure many of our meats and fish in-house, and the process can be time-consuming. This method results in similar flavors to home curing but isn't quite so involved. The sauce has been a family favorite for a long time, and now it's a L'Espalier favorite. Aunt Midge is my great-great-aunt, and she devised this recipe to go with salmon. We serve it with any kind of fish or shellfish.

¼ cup kosher salt

1 cup granulated sugar

¼ cup brown sugar

1 teaspoon ground fennel

1 teaspoon ground coriander

¼ teaspoon ground cloves

1 bay leaf, crushed

1 teaspoon caraway seeds

1 teaspoon lemon zest

1 teaspoon lime zest

1 teaspoon orange zest

1 teaspoon dried mint

1 pound salmon fillets (skin on)

1 tablespoon canola oil

1 Combine the salt, sugars, fennel, coriander, cloves, bay leaf, caraway seeds, citrus zests, and mint in a small bowl. Place the salmon fillets, skin side down, on a plate. Evenly distribute the curing mixture over the surface of the salmon, covering all the flesh. Refrigerate the salmon, covered, and let cure for 4 hours or overnight.

2 Preheat the oven to 400°F.

3 Remove the salmon from the refrigerator. Rinse the curing mixture off the fillets and pat them dry with paper towels. Divide the salmon into 6 equal-sized portions.

4 Place a medium-size ovenproof sauté pan over medium-high heat for 3 to 4 minutes. Add the canola oil and heat for about 1 minute. Place the salmon, skin side down, in the pan and cook for 1 minute. Transfer the pan to the oven and roast the salmon for 4 minutes per ½ inch of thickness for medium doneness.

5 To serve, place 1 tablespoon of Aunt Midge's Sauce (page 56) on each of 6 plates. Divide the Mustard Greens (page 56) evenly among the plates, placing them next to the sauce, leaving room for the salmon. Carefully position the salmon next to the sauce and the greens.

Aunt Midge's Sauce

4 tablespoons mayonnaise

4 tablespoons crème fraîche

1 teaspoon Dijon mustard

½ teaspoon prepared
 horseradish or ½ teaspoon
 prepared wasabi

½ teaspoon Worcestershire
 sauce

1 teaspoon dried *fines herbes*
 (below)

1 tablespoon sherry

½ teaspoon cayenne pepper

Salt

Combine the mayonnaise, crème fraîche, mustard, horseradish, Worcestershire sauce, *fines herbes*, sherry, cayenne, and salt to taste in a food processor or blender until smooth. The sauce will keep in the refrigerator for up to 3 days.

Mustard Greens

¼ pound (about 3 cups) mustard
 greens

Salt and freshly ground black
 pepper

1 tablespoon fresh lemon juice

2 tablespoons extra virgin olive
 oil

Place the greens in a large bowl and season with salt and pepper. Whisk together the lemon juice and olive oil in a small bowl and season with salt and pepper to taste. Toss with the greens.

FINES HERBES

Fines herbes refers to a mix of parsley, tarragon, chervil, and chives that is a staple in French cooking. You should be able to find dried *fines herbes* on your supermarket spice rack, but if you can't, you can substitute a mixture of equal parts parsley flakes and dried tarragon.

Crispy Confit Duck Hash with Black Kale and Poached Eggs

This recipe uses L'Espalier's version of confit duck—it's a house specialty. Our preparation method brings out the best of the sweetness in the duck. Black kale also often goes by the names dinosaur kale or Tuscan kale. The poached eggs are great with this menu, on their own, or with a little Citrus Hollandaise (page 28) spooned on top. If you don't want to make your own confit, you can usually find it at specialty butcher shops (that's also a good place to look for duck fat if you do want to make your own).

1 tablespoon butter

1 tablespoon olive oil

1 large yellow onion, diced

1 leek, sliced in half, washed (page 195), and diced

2 garlic cloves, minced

1 sweet potato, peeled and diced into ¼-inch cubes

2 celery stalks, diced

1 medium-size red bell pepper, seeded and diced

Confit Duck (page 58)

1 tablespoon fresh thyme leaves

1 tablespoon balsamic vinegar

1 tablespoon port

1 teaspoon Worcestershire sauce

1 Heat a medium-size sauté pan over medium-high heat for 2 minutes. Add the butter and oil to the pan. When the butter starts to sizzle, add the onion and leek. Stir with a wooden spoon and cook for about 3 minutes, until translucent. Add the garlic and stir for 30 seconds. Add the sweet potato, celery, and red bell pepper and stir them in; reduce the heat to low and cover. Cook for 10 minutes, or until the sweet potatoes are tender enough to pierce easily with a knife.

2 Uncover and add the confit duck and the thyme. Stir until evenly mixed. Turn the heat to medium and add the vinegar, port, and Worcestershire sauce. Cook for 3 more minutes.

3 Scoop the hash onto a serving platter, and place a bed of Black Kale (page 59) at the center of the platter, on top of the hash. Arrange the Poached Eggs (page 59) over the top of the kale.

Confit Duck

2 tablespoons salt

1 tablespoon brown sugar

½ teaspoon ground allspice

¼ teaspoon ground cloves

1 tablespoon dried rosemary

1 teaspoon dried thyme

6 juniper berries, crushed with
   the flat end of a knife

1 bay leaf, crushed

Zest of 1 orange

4 duck legs

1 quart duck fat or vegetable oil

1 Combine the salt, sugar, allspice, cloves, rosemary, thyme, juniper berries, bay leaf, and orange zest in a medium-size bowl. Toss the duck legs with the mixture until evenly coated. Refrigerate, covered, for at least 4 hours or, for best results, overnight.

2 Preheat the oven to 325°F.

3 Place the duck legs in a large ovenproof pot and cover with the duck fat. Heat over medium-high heat for 5 minutes, or until the duck fat begins to simmer.

4 Cover the pot and put it in the oven to bake for about 3 hours, or until a fork moves through the meat effortlessly. Allow the duck to cool until it's just warm to the touch, and then remove it from the duck fat. You could serve it as is and impress your guests with straight-up confit duck—or remove the meat from the bones and set aside to use in the Crispy Confit Duck Hash.

Black Kale

1 tablespoon butter

1 tablespoon olive oil

1 small yellow onion, diced

2 garlic cloves, minced

½ pound (2 bunches) black kale, roughly chopped

1 tablespoon fresh lemon juice

1 teaspoon dried tarragon

Salt and freshly ground black pepper

1 Heat a large pot over medium-high heat for 2 minutes. Add the butter and oil. When the butter is sizzling (that should take about 1 minute), add the onion and garlic and cook until the onion is translucent, about 3 minutes.

2 Add the kale and cover. Reduce the heat to medium and cook for 2 minutes. Stir in the lemon juice and tarragon and cook for 3 minutes. Stir again. Cover and cook for about 3 more minutes, until tender. Season with salt and pepper.

Poached Eggs

1 tablespoon salt, plus more to taste

1 tablespoon white vinegar

2 whole black peppercorns

6 large eggs

Freshly ground black pepper

1 Fill a large saucepan halfway with water. Add the salt, vinegar, and peppercorns. Bring the water to a simmer over medium-low heat.

2 Crack the eggs into the simmering water. Cook for 5 to 6 minutes, until the whites are completely cooked. Remove the eggs from the water with a slotted spoon. Season with salt and pepper.

Roasted Peppered Venison with Red Currant–Zinfandel Sauce and Celery Root and Parsnips

Venison is leaner and healthier than many meats, and it has a wonderful and distinctive gamey flavor. The earthiness of celery root and parsnips comple- ments the venison perfectly in this winter dish. You can roast the celery root and parsnips while the venison rack is cooling. Just turn the oven temperature up to 400°F when you remove the venison. Fresh currants are readily available in supermarkets in the fall and winter.

Red Currant–Zinfandel Marinade
  (recipe follows)

1 venison rack (about 3 pounds)

2 celery stalks, chopped

1 yellow onion, chopped

2 carrots, peeled and coarsely
  chopped

1 leek, washed (page 195) and
  coarsely chopped

1 cup fresh red currants

1 teaspoon dried thyme

4 garlic cloves, crushed

2 bay leaves

1 whole clove

1 cup Zinfandel

½ cup fresh orange juice

2 slices bacon

1 Spread the marinade evenly over the venison rack. Let marinate, covered, in the refrigera- tor for 3 hours or overnight. Remove the rack from the refrigerator at least 1 hour prior to cooking.

2 Preheat the oven to 450°F.

3 Combine the celery, onion, carrots, leek, ¾ cup of the currants, the thyme, garlic, bay leaves, clove, wine, and orange juice in a roasting pan. Place the pan in the oven to heat just before searing the venison.

4 Heat a large cast-iron skillet over medium heat for about 2 minutes. Add the bacon to the pan and cook until the fat is rendered, about 8 minutes. Remove the bacon from the skillet and set aside. When cool enough, chop the bacon into small bits.

5 Place the venison rack, meat side down, in the skillet, and turn the heat up to high. Cook the rack until it's browned evenly on all sides, about 4 minutes total.

6 Transfer the rack to the roasting pan and reduce the oven temperature to 325°F. Roast for 20 minutes, or until the internal temperature of the meat is 132° to 135°F (for rare), or another 2 to 4 minutes for medium-rare (136° to 140°F). Transfer the rack to a platter and cover it with aluminum foil, allowing it to rest for at least 15 minutes before carving.

7 Meanwhile, strain all the juices from the roasting pan through a fine-mesh sieve into a large saucepan. Reduce the liquid by half over medium heat, about 4 minutes. Add the remaining ¼ cup currants and the bacon. Spoon the sauce over the venison and serve with the Celery Root and Parsnips (page 62).

Red Currant–Zinfandel Marinade

½ cup fresh red currants

2 tablespoons Dijon mustard

2 shallots, minced

2 garlic cloves, minced

5 juniper berries

1 teaspoon dried thyme

2 bay leaves

1 teaspoon dried rosemary

3 tablespoons Zinfandel

2 tablespoons canola oil

1 teaspoon freshly ground black pepper

Combine the currants, mustard, shallots, garlic, juniper berries, thyme, bay leaves, rosemary, wine, oil, and pepper in a food processor and blend until smooth.

2 celery roots, peeled and cut into ½-inch sticks

4 parsnips, peeled and quartered lengthwise

1 tablespoon *herbes de Provence* (page 31)

1 teaspoon salt

1 teaspoon freshly ground black pepper

2 tablespoons canola oil

1 Preheat the oven to 400°F.

2 Toss the celery root and parsnip pieces with the *herbes de Provence*, salt, and pepper in a bowl.

3 Heat a large cast-iron skillet over high heat for 3 minutes. Add the oil to the pan and heat for 1 minute. Evenly distribute the vegetables over the surface of the pan and cook, stirring, for 3 to 4 minutes.

4 Transfer the skillet to the oven and roast for 20 minutes, or until the vegetables are golden brown.

ROOTING AROUND

Try this preparation with other root vegetables, such as carrots, turnips, sweet potatoes, or rutabagas.

Ricotta Tarts with Pine Nuts and Cocoa Nibs

Creamy, slightly citrusy, and not too heavy, this dessert is a delicious way to finish off a winter meal along with a glass of port. Cocoa nibs are being used more and more often in restaurant desserts, and with good reason. They are roasted cocoa beans that have been separated from their husks and broken into pieces, and they have a subtle, but unadulterated, chocolate flavor. You can easily find them in gourmet stores, chocolate shops, and online.

1 recipe Pâte Real (page 42)

2 cups whole-milk ricotta cheese

½ cup buttermilk

½ cup heavy cream

⅔ cup sugar

1 teaspoon pure vanilla extract

Zest of 1 orange

Zest of 1 lemon

¼ teaspoon ground nutmeg

½ teaspoon salt

4 large egg yolks

1 large egg

¼ cup pine nuts

¼ cup cocoa nibs

1　Preheat the oven to 350°F.

2　Divide the pastry dough into 6 portions and press the dough into 6 individual 3½-inch tart pans. (If you prefer to make one large tart, use a 10-inch tart pan.) Place the tart pans or pan on a baking sheet and bake for 12 minutes.

3　In a large bowl, beat together the ricotta, buttermilk, cream, sugar, vanilla, orange and lemon zests, nutmeg, salt, egg yolks, and egg. Pour the mixture into the parbaked crusts. Evenly distribute the pine nuts and cocoa nibs over the tops of the tarts. Bake for 15 minutes (or 20 minutes for a 10-inch tart), until the top of the filling is just starting to crack. Let cool on a wire rack for at least 15 minutes before serving.

SPRING

ROSÉ-COLORED GLASSES

My travels have taken me to Provence many times, and one of my favorite things to do there is to visit the roving food markets and shop for produce, meats, fish, olives, and bread to make dinner for the day. During the shopping trips we always make time to stop and enjoy my favorite bottle of rosé (whatever that happens to be at the moment) with a three-course lunch. I have adored rosé for years, and so has our wine director, Erik Johnson. For a long time when we talked about rosé we sounded like Red Sox fans (before they won the World Series) at the start of yet another season. "This is the year," we'd say. "This is the year rosé will really take off." Around the same time that the Sox finally did win the Series again, in 2004, it happened. Is it a coincidence? We don't know. But in the past few years, rosé has come into its own in the public eye and really been embraced. People used to perceive it as an overly sweet, unsophisticated wine, but nothing could be further from the truth. It's incredible with all kinds of food, and it combines the best of red and white wines—the great red fruit flavors and the herbaceous and mineral flavors of white. There are a lot of great rosés out there, so start trying them and experimenting to see what you like.

MENU

& pairings

↓

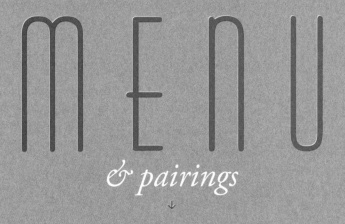

 +

PAIRINGS

Broth of Escargots, Ramps, and Morels	**1**	**Louis Bouillot, "Perle d'Aurore," Rosé Brut, Crémant de Bourgogne, France**
Poached Halibut à la Provençale	**2**	**2006 Château de Roquefort, "Corail," Rosé, Côtes de Provence, France**
Pot-Roasted Pork with Chorizo and Clams	**3**	**2006 Villa Gemma, "Cerasuolo," Rosé, Montepulciano d'Abruzzo, Italy**
Strawberry Soup with Crème Fraîche Chantilly	**4**	**Château de Beaulon, 10-Year "Vieille Réserve Ruby," Pineau des Charentes, Cognac, France**

WINE 🍾 NOTES

↓

1ST PAIRING **BROTH OF ESCARGOTS, RAMPS, AND MORELS**
SERVED WITH → **LOUIS BOUILLOT, "PERLE D'AURORE," ROSÉ BRUT, CRÉMANT DE BOURGOGNE, FRANCE**

It's always nice to start with bubbles. It creates a party atmosphere no matter what the occasion. Good sparkling rosé is fantastic—dry and crisp, with subtle berry flavors. But good sparkling rosé isn't always easy to find. This is one we love. If you can't find a good one, a dry sparkling wine from Alsace or California (or Champagne, of course) would be delicious with this dish.

2ND PAIRING **POACHED HALIBUT À LA PROVENÇALE**
SERVED WITH → **2006 CHÂTEAU DE ROQUEFORT, "CORAIL," ROSÉ, CÔTES DE PROVENCE, FRANCE**

Here we pair a rosé from Provence—the ultimate source of good rosé—with a Provençal dish. This is a light rosé, but not too light. It has a hint of earthiness but won't overpower the fish. Try any medium-bodied rosé from Provence here.

3RD PAIRING **POT-ROASTED PORK WITH CHORIZO AND CLAMS**
SERVED WITH → **2006 VILLA GEMMA, "CERASUOLO," ROSÉ, MONTEPULCIANO D'ABRUZZO, ITALY**

This is about as dark and burly as a rosé gets. It's great with the spiciness of the chorizo. Another dark, full rosé would also be nice.

4TH PAIRING **STRAWBERRY SOUP WITH CRÈME FRAÎCHE CHANTILLY**
SERVED WITH → **CHÂTEAU DE BEAULON, 10-YEAR "VIEILLE RÉSERVE RUBY,"
PINEAU DES CHARENTES, COGNAC, FRANCE**

A combination of white wine and Cognac, this is a sweet wine that's great with dessert or served as an apéritif. A Muscat de Beaumes-de-Venise would be another nice pairing with the Strawberry Soup.

Broth of Escargots, Ramps, and Morels

The brightness of rosé on the palate cuts the richness of the snails and the ramps and helps all the ingredients to taste amazing. Escargots are readily available at gourmet food shops, in many large grocery stores, and online. They are easy to work with, so don't be intimidated by the idea of cooking them at home. Ramps are a type of wild onion that are widely available in spring; if you can't find them, you can substitute scallions.

2 tablespoons olive oil

1 Vidalia onion, chopped

3 garlic cloves, minced

1 cup white wine

¼ cup sweet sherry

1 cup vegetable broth

2 tablespoons butter

4 ounces fresh morels, or 2 ounces dried, reconstituted morels (page 91), sliced lengthwise if very large

12 ramps, washed (page 93) and trimmed

24 escargots, washed and drained

1 tablespoon chopped fresh flat-leaf parsley

1 tablespoon chopped fresh chives

1 teaspoon fresh thyme leaves

¼ teaspoon ground nutmeg

½ teaspoon fresh lemon juice

¼ cup heavy cream

Salt and freshly ground black pepper

1   Heat a large saucepan over medium heat and add the olive oil. When the oil is hot, add the onion and cook until translucent, 3 to 4 minutes. Add the garlic and cook for an additional 2 minutes. Add the wine, sherry, and broth and bring to a simmer. Remove from the heat and puree in a blender until smooth.

2   Wipe out the saucepan and place it over medium-low heat. Melt the butter in the pan, then add the morels, ramps, and escargots. Cover the pan and cook for 5 minutes, stirring occasionally. Add the pureed broth to the pan and bring to a simmer. Add the parsley, chives, thyme, nutmeg, and lemon juice. Stir in the cream and bring back to a simmer for 1 minute. Season with salt and pepper. Serve immediately.

Poached Halibut à la Provençale

This is a wonderful way to use ingredients that return to the market in the spring after a long winter. When the sun is higher in the sky I look to the Mediterranean for cooking inspiration, and I crave lots of vegetables. Halibut is also at its best in the spring.

¼ cup plus 3 tablespoons olive oil

1 Vidalia onion, diced

6 garlic cloves, minced

2 small zucchini, diced

1 large red bell pepper, seeded and diced

2 large tomatoes, peeled (page 123), seeded, and diced

1 fennel bulb, diced, feathery top reserved

Six 3-ounce halibut fillets

Zest of 1 orange

Zest of 1 lemon

Salt and freshly ground black pepper

1 cup white wine

3 shallots, minced

¼ cup dry sherry

1 tablespoon minced fresh flat-leaf parsley

1 teaspoon minced fresh chives

Juice of 1 lemon

1 Preheat the oven to 350°F.

2 To prepare the vegetables, heat a large sauté pan on medium-high and add ¼ cup oil. When the oil is hot, add the onion and cook for 3 minutes. Add 4 of the minced garlic cloves, the zucchini, red pepper, tomatoes, and diced fennel and cook for 4 minutes. Transfer to a platter.

3 Place the halibut fillets in a bowl and toss them gently with the remaining 3 tablespoons olive oil and the orange and lemon zests. Season with salt and pepper. Place the fillets in a large braising pan. Add the wine, shallots, the remaining 2 minced garlic cloves, the sherry, parsley, chives, and lemon juice and cook on medium heat for 4 minutes. Cover the pan and bake in the oven for 12 to 14 minutes.

4 Remove the fillets from the oven and transfer them with a slotted spoon onto the vegetables on the platter. Garnish with a few fronds of the reserved fennel top. Strain the sauce from the braising pan through a fine-mesh sieve into a small serving bowl or sauceboat. Serve with the halibut.

Pot-Roasted Pork with Chorizo and Clams

The sweetness of the clams and the spiciness of the chorizo are a wonderful and classic combination. A full-bodied rosé incorporates the whole spice rack, the flavors of a light red, and the minerality of a white, so it goes well with a dish that features such a variety of tastes. Letting the pork absorb a quick homemade dry rub overnight gives it even more delicious flavor. We make this with pork shoulder, which is sometimes called pork butt—so if that's what your butcher calls it, don't be afraid to buy it.

¼ cup salt

¼ cup brown sugar

1 teaspoon crushed red pepper

1 teaspoon ground cumin

1 teaspoon ground allspice

4 pounds pork shoulder

3 tablespoons vegetable oil

1 onion, diced

2 leeks, halved, washed (page 195), and diced

2 carrots, peeled and diced

2 celery stalks, diced

5 garlic cloves, chopped

½ cup golden raisins

One 750-ml bottle dry rosé

1 cup chicken or vegetable broth

1 link Spanish (smoked) chorizo, cut into small pieces

1 Combine the salt, brown sugar, red pepper, cumin, and allspice. Rub the mixture all over the pork. Place the rubbed pork in a bowl and cover tightly with plastic wrap. Refrigerate overnight. Remove the pork from the refrigerator 2 hours before cooking.

2 Preheat the oven to 325°F.

3 Remove the pork from the bowl and pat dry with paper towels. Heat a large roasting pan over medium-high heat for 3 minutes. Add the vegetable oil and heat for 1 minute. Add the pork to the pan and brown it on all sides, turning often, about 4 minutes total. Remove the pork from the pan and set aside.

4 Reduce the heat to medium, add the onion, and stir with a wooden spoon for 3 minutes. Add the leeks, carrots, and celery and sauté for 3 minutes. Add the garlic and raisins and cook for 1 minute. Add the rosé, broth, and chorizo and return the pork to the pan. Cover and bake for 3½ hours.

(continued)

18 littleneck clams, rinsed

2 teaspoons finely minced fresh rosemary

2 teaspoons fresh oregano

2 tablespoons finely minced fresh flat-leaf parsley

Salt and freshly ground black pepper

5 Remove from the oven and place the pork on a serving platter to rest. Place the pan over medium heat and add the clams, rosemary, oregano, and 1 tablespoon of the parsley. Cover and cook for 3½ to 4½ minutes, or until the clams open (discard any clams that do not open). Taste for seasoning and add salt and pepper if desired. Arrange the clams around the pork on the platter.

6 Ladle ⅓ cup of the chorizo-raisin broth over the pork and clams. Pour the remaining broth from the roasting pan into a small serving bowl. Serve the pork in broad-rimmed bowls, with a slice of pork in the center, clams around the sides, and roasting broth ladled on top. Garnish with the remaining 1 tablespoon parsley.

HOMEMADE CRÈME FRAÎCHE

It's very easy and inexpensive to make your own crème fraîche. Sanitize a nonreactive container in your dishwasher. Combine 1½ teaspoons buttermilk with ½ cup heavy cream, cover with cheesecloth or a clean kitchen towel, and let stand at room temperature for 24 hours.

Strawberry Soup with Crème Fraîche Chantilly

I have made this soup since the beginning of my career, when I worked at Harvest restaurant in Cambridge, Massachusetts. I loved it then, and it's something I still make every spring. Ideally, you should complement the soup with anise hyssop, which is one of my favorite herbs. It has an unusual anise-mint flavor, and you can find it at stores that stock a good variety of culinary herbs. It's a perennial, and it's wonderful to have in your garden. If you can't find it, use mint.

9 cups fresh strawberries (about 3½ pounds), washed (page 118), hulled, and halved

¾ cup sugar

1 tablespoon minced fresh anise hyssop or mint

1 Toss the strawberries with the sugar. Cook them gently in the top portion of a double boiler, or in a heatproof bowl set over a pan of hot water (make sure the water is just hot, not boiling), for 1 hour. Strain through a fine-mesh sieve, reserving the liquid and the berries.

2 Refrigerate the liquid until all the solids fall to the bottom of the container. Ladle the clear soup off the top and discard the sediment on the bottom. Chill until ready to serve.

3 Toss the reserved berries with the anise hyssop. Serve the soup in bowls topped with a spoonful of berries and a dollop of Crème Fraîche Chantilly (recipe follows).

Crème Fraîche Chantilly

6 tablespoons crème fraîche (facing page)

½ cup heavy cream

2 tablespoons sugar

Zest of 1 lemon

Combine the crème fraîche, heavy cream, sugar, and lemon zest in a bowl and whip with an electric mixer until soft peaks form.

AUSTRALIA AND NEW ZEALAND

New World wines from Australia and New Zealand continue to astonish me with their quality. My first recollection of a New Zealand Sauvignon Blanc is from more than 10 years ago. I drank Cloudy Bay Sauvignon Blanc with some Malpeque oysters, and it was an almost religious experience. But Sauvignon Blanc isn't the only wine from this part of the globe. I'm a huge fan of Shiraz from Australia, too. It's some of the best in the world and it matches beautifully with many foods, from seafood to meats.

MENU

& pairings

↓

 +

PAIRINGS

Oysters on the Half Shell with Seaweed Salad, Sherry Mignonette, and Caviar

1

2004 Two Hands, "The Wolf," Riesling, Clare Valley, Australia

Alaskan King Salmon with Black Quinoa and Cherries

2

2004 Mt. Difficulty, Pinot Noir, Central Otago, New Zealand

Walnut-Encrusted Spring Lamb with Bacon-Potato Rösti

3

2003 Grant Burge, "Miamba," Shiraz, Barossa Valley, Australia

Coconut Tapioca with Candied Basil

4

2002 De Bortoli, "Noble One," Sémillon, Yarra Valley, Australia

WINE 🍷 NOTES

↓

1ST PAIRING **OYSTERS ON THE HALF SHELL WITH SEAWEED SALAD, SHERRY MIGNONETTE, AND CAVIAR**
SERVED WITH → **2004 TWO HANDS, "THE WOLF," RIESLING, CLARE VALLEY, AUSTRALIA**

This is a dry Riesling, racy and crisp. Many people expect Riesling to be sweet, but Rieslings from Australia and Alsace are generally drier than those from Germany. Another dry Riesling from Australia, Alsace, or the Pacific Northwest, or a New Zealand Sauvignon Blanc, will also complement these oysters.

2ND PAIRING **ALASKAN KING SALMON WITH BLACK QUINOA AND CHERRIES**
SERVED WITH → **2004 MT. DIFFICULTY, PINOT NOIR, CENTRAL OTAGO, NEW ZEALAND**

Marlborough is New Zealand's largest wine region; Central Otago is the other big one. We think New Zealand will soon become famous for its Pinot Noir. The climate is sunny but still cool, perfect for Pinot—which is terrific with salmon. Any good Pinot Noir pairs well with this dish.

3RD PAIRING **WALNUT-ENCRUSTED SPRING LAMB WITH BACON-POTATO RÖSTI**
SERVED WITH → **2003 GRANT BURGE, "MIAMBA," SHIRAZ, BAROSSA VALLEY, AUSTRALIA**

Full, rich, and spicy, this is a classic Australian red wine. Shiraz and lamb is an excellent combination. You could try a Shiraz from South Africa or a California Syrah, too.

4TH PAIRING **COCONUT TAPIOCA WITH CANDIED BASIL**
SERVED WITH → **2002 DE BORTOLI, "NOBLE ONE," SÉMILLON, YARRA VALLEY, AUSTRALIA**

Sémillon is the main grape varietal in Sauternes; this selection is a classic Sauternes-style dessert wine from Australia. So naturally you could sub a Sauternes here, or a California wine made from Sémillon grapes.

Oysters on the Half Shell
with Seaweed Salad,
Sherry Mignonette, and Caviar

For anyone who loves oysters, this is a dream-come-true dish. It combines the brininess of the oysters, the salt of the caviar, and the salty-sweet taste of the seaweed salad with a mignonette that incorporates the tartness of vinegar and the light, fruity, herbaceous qualities of Riesling. Use whatever kind of caviar you like—sturgeon, golden, salmon, etc.

24 oysters, shucked

4 ounces store-bought seaweed salad

Sherry Mignonette (recipe follows)

1 ounce American caviar of your choice

Place 4 oysters on each of 6 plates. Divide the seaweed salad evenly among the plates, placing it on top of each oyster. Spoon a little mignonette on each oyster, then top with the caviar.

Sherry Mignonette

3 tablespoons aged sherry vinegar

1 tablespoon dry Riesling

1 shallot, minced

Salt and cracked black pepper

Whisk together the vinegar, wine, shallot, salt, and pepper until well combined.

Alaskan King Salmon with Black Quinoa and Cherries

The nuttiness of the quinoa and the dark cherry flavor work well with the Pinot Noir and the buttery richness of the salmon. In fact, salmon is one of my favorite things to have with Pinot Noir. Who says you must have white wine with fish, anyway? Not me.

¼ cup (½ stick) butter

¼ cup olive oil

2 tablespoons fresh lemon juice

1 teaspoon minced fresh rosemary

1 tablespoon chopped fresh chives

1 tablespoon chopped fresh flat-leaf parsley

1 tablespoon chopped fresh chervil leaves

2 garlic cloves, minced

2 shallots, coarsely chopped

One 1½-pound salmon fillet

Salt and freshly ground black pepper

Fresh cherries (optional, for garnish)

6 sprigs fresh chervil (optional, for garnish)

1   Preheat the oven to 350°F.

2   Combine the butter, olive oil, lemon juice, rosemary, chives, parsley, chervil, garlic, and shallots in a medium-size saucepan and cook over low heat until the butter has melted.

3   Place the salmon, skin side down, in a baking dish. Pour the butter mixture evenly over the salmon. Season with salt and pepper and cover the dish with aluminum foil. Bake for 12 minutes.

4   Remove the salmon from the oven and lift it onto a cutting board. Cut it into 6 equal pieces. Place on serving plates and spoon the baking juices over the pieces. Garnish with fresh cherries and a sprig of chervil, if desired, and serve with Black Quinoa and Cherries (recipe follows).

Black Quinoa and Cherries

1 cup black quinoa (below)

2 tablespoons butter

1 small yellow onion, diced

2 garlic cloves, minced

1 celery stalk, peeled and diced

2 cups vegetable broth

½ cup white wine

1 teaspoon fresh thyme

1 bay leaf

¼ cup heavy cream

2 tablespoons freshly grated
  Parmesan cheese

1 tablespoon fresh lemon juice

¼ teaspoon ground nutmeg

1½ cups pitted and chopped
  cherries

Salt and freshly ground black
  pepper

1 Preheat the oven to 350°F.

2 Place the quinoa in a dry, medium-size saucepan over low heat and toast for 10 to 15 minutes, stirring constantly (the quinoa should get somewhat lighter in color). Remove from the heat and set aside.

3 Melt the butter in a medium-size ovenproof pot over medium heat. Add the onion and cook for 3 minutes. Add the garlic and celery and cook for 1 minute. Pour the toasted quinoa into the pot. Add the broth, wine, thyme, and bay leaf.

4 Cover and bake for 45 minutes, or until the quinoa has cracked and expanded, or "bloomed." Remove from the oven and add the heavy cream, cheese, lemon juice, and nutmeg, and mix thoroughly. Add the cherries and season with salt and pepper to taste.

BLACK QUINOA

Black quinoa is sweeter and nuttier in flavor than regular quinoa. It's getting easier to find and is available at Whole Foods stores and online. You can substitute regular quinoa if you can't find the black variety.

Walnut-Encrusted Spring Lamb
with Bacon-Potato Rösti

This has been a L'Espalier staple for decades. The nuttiness and sweetness of the crust enhances the richness and sweetness of the spring lamb. The rösti lends crispness to this dish and creates a platform to absorb the sweet juices from the lamb. To add a green element to this course, serve it with spring spinach.

3 tablespoons balsamic vinegar

3 tablespoons Dijon mustard

3 garlic cloves, minced

3 tablespoons olive oil, plus
  more if needed

1 teaspoon dried thyme

1 teaspoon dried rosemary

2 racks of lamb (about 18 ounces
  total)

3 tablespoons butter

1 large onion, thinly sliced

1 tablespoon brown sugar

2 teaspoons salt, plus more to
  season lamb

4 garlic cloves, chopped

4 teaspoons minced fresh
  rosemary

2 teaspoons minced fresh mint

1 cup walnuts, lightly toasted
  (page 171)

¼ cup breadcrumbs

1 teaspoon coarse sea salt

1 teaspoon freshly ground black
  pepper, plus more to season
  lamb

1 tablespoon sherry vinegar

2 tablespoons vegetable oil

1 Make a marinade by combining the balsamic vinegar, mustard, minced garlic, 2 tablespoons of the olive oil, the thyme, and the dried rosemary. Place the lamb in a bowl and smear the marinade all over the meat. Refrigerate, covered, overnight.

2 Heat a large sauté pan over medium heat. Add the butter to the pan. When the butter is sizzling, add the onions, brown sugar, and salt and stir. Cover and let cook for 10 minutes.

3 Uncover and add the chopped garlic, fresh rosemary, mint, walnuts, breadcrumbs, salt, pepper, 1 tablespoon olive oil, and sherry vinegar. Stir and cook for 3 minutes. Remove from the heat and puree in a food processor until smooth. If the mixture crumbles, add more olive oil. (You want to be able to apply the mixture to the lamb with an offset spatula.)

4 Preheat the oven to 400°F.

5 Remove the lamb from the marinade. Season the lamb with salt and pepper. Wipe out the sauté pan and set it over medium-high heat. Add the vegetable oil to the pan. When the oil is hot, add the lamb to the pan and brown it deeply on all sides, about 4 minutes total.

6 Place the lamb on a roasting rack in a roasting pan. Use an offset spatula to cover the lamb completely with the walnut-herb mixture. Roast for about 12 minutes for medium-rare (about 135°F on an instant-read thermometer). Remove from the oven and let stand for 5 minutes before slicing and serving. Serve with Bacon-Potato Rösti (recipe follows).

Bacon-Potato Rösti

3 Idaho potatoes (about 2½ pounds), peeled

2 slices bacon, finely diced

1 tablespoon salt

1 garlic clove, minced

3 tablespoons minced onion

½ teaspoon freshly ground black pepper

¼ cup (½ stick) butter

1 Grate the potatoes, using the large holes of a grater, into a large bowl. Let stand for 4 minutes. Lift the potatoes and squeeze out and discard the excess liquid. Return the potatoes to the bowl and stir in the bacon. Mix in the salt, garlic, onion, and pepper.

2 Preheat the oven to 400°F.

3 Heat a large ovenproof skillet over medium heat. Add 2 tablespoons of the butter to the skillet and, when it starts to pop, evenly distribute the potato-bacon mixture in the skillet. Let cook until the potato cake becomes golden brown and begins to detach from the pan, 8 to 10 minutes.

4 Distribute the remaining 2 tablespoons butter, cut into bits, on top of the potato cake. Flip the cake and place the skillet in the oven. Roast for 15 minutes. Remove the rösti from the skillet and slide it onto a cutting board. Cut it into 6 wedges and serve with the lamb.

Coconut Tapioca with Candied Basil

Tapioca was one of my favorite desserts when I was growing up, and my grand-mother always made it for me. I've always loved the texture, and I still crave it today. This recipe is one of several tributes in this book to the food of my childhood memories, which are, of course, deeply ingrained in my approach to cooking. For the Candied Basil, I prefer to use Thai basil, but regular basil will also work.

1 cup tapioca, soaked in water
   overnight

2 cups milk

5 cups coconut milk

2 tablespoons sugar

1 teaspoon salt

1 Strain the tapioca. Combine the milk, coconut milk, sugar, and salt in a medium-size saucepan over low heat. Add the tapioca to the pan, bring to a simmer, and simmer for 20 minutes. Remove from the heat and chill over an ice bath (page 21).

2 Refrigerate for at least 2 hours, or until the tapioca sets. (The tapioca will keep for a few days, covered, in the refrigerator.) Serve with Candied Basil (recipe follows).

Candied Basil

½ cup sugar

2½ tablespoons water

16 fresh basil leaves, washed
   and thoroughly dried

1 Preheat the oven to 175°F.

2 Combine the sugar and water in a small saucepan over low heat until the sugar has completely dissolved. Remove from the heat and let cool so that it's just warm (not hot, or the basil will discolor). Soak the basil leaves in the syrup for 5 minutes.

3 Remove the leaves from the syrup and place them on a baking sheet lined with parchment paper. Bake for 10 minutes, or until crystallized.

PICNIC BASKET GOODIES

There are many ways to interpret the picnic basket. This menu definitely takes an elegant approach, but it still features fun and accessible foods: a club sandwich, pasta salad, barbecued chicken, potato salad, and chocolate cake. Inviting friends for a picnic (whether it's indoors or out) sets a festive tone, and pairing sparkling wine with the first course guarantees a party atmosphere.

MENU

& pairings

↓

 +

PAIRINGS

Maine Lobster and Avocado Club Sandwich with Smoked Paprika Potato Chips	**1**	Nino Franco, "Rustico," Prosecco di Valdobbiadene, Italy
Porcini Ravioli with Pea Pesto	**2**	2002 Ludwig Neumayer, Grüner Veltliner, Traisental, Austria
Barbecued Chicken with Grilled Ramps and Blue Potato Salad	**3**	2003 Domaine du Vissoux, "Cuvée Traditionnelle," Beaujolais, France
Chocolate Hazelnut Tortes	**4**	Emilio Lustau, "East India Solera," Cream Sherry, Andalucía, Spain

WINE 📖 NOTES

↓

1ST PAIRING **MAINE LOBSTER AND AVOCADO CLUB SANDWICH WITH SMOKED PAPRIKA POTATO CHIPS**
SERVED WITH → **NINO FRANCO, "RUSTICO," PROSECCO DI VALDOBBIADENE, ITALY**

Prosecco is the sparkling wine of Italy, and it's widely available and affordable. This one is dry with a lemony and nutty flavor. Another dry prosecco or a dry Champagne would be delicious with the sweet lobster and rich avocado in this sandwich.

2ND PAIRING **PORCINI RAVIOLI WITH PEA PESTO**
SERVED WITH → **2002 LUDWIG NEUMAYER, GRÜNER VELTLINER, TRAISENTAL, AUSTRIA**

Grüner Veltliner is one of the native grape varieties of Austria. This one isn't too heavy—it's bright and fresh with a hint of white pepper. The earthiness of the mushrooms and sweetness of the peas go well with the spice in the wine. Try any Grüner Veltliner if you can't find this one.

3RD PAIRING **BARBECUED CHICKEN WITH GRILLED RAMPS AND BLUE POTATO SALAD**
SERVED WITH → **2003 DOMAINE DU VISSOUX, "CUVÉE TRADITIONNELLE," BEAUJOLAIS, FRANCE**

Beaujolais gets a bad rap because of Beaujolais Nouveau, but it's really a fun wine. It's aged for a short time, light, and not too complex, which is just what it's supposed to be. This one is a little fuller than most, but any good Beaujolais would work here (Beaujolais and chicken is a classic pairing), as would a nice Pinot Noir.

4TH PAIRING **CHOCOLATE HAZELNUT TORTES**
SERVED WITH → **EMILIO LUSTAU, "EAST INDIA SOLERA," CREAM SHERRY, ANDALUCÍA, SPAIN**

This cream-style sherry is sweet and rich, not zippy or tart. Chocolate finales are good with a wine that's sweeter than the dessert, so definitely choose a sweet dessert wine here.

Maine Lobster and Avocado Club Sandwich with Smoked Paprika Potato Chips

The classic New England lobster roll meets the club in this decadent sandwich that's sure to become a favorite. We cut the sandwiches in half and serve each person one of the halves as a first course; you could, of course, make more sandwiches and turn them into the main part of your meal.

1 small loaf sourdough bread, cut into 6 slices

2 teaspoons olive oil

1 garlic clove, crushed

6 slices bacon

1 pound cooked lobster meat, coarsely chopped

⅓ cup mayonnaise

¼ teaspoon ground chipotle chile pepper

½ teaspoon Worcestershire sauce

1 tablespoon fresh lemon juice

¼ cup finely chopped fresh tarragon

Salt and freshly ground black pepper

1 small red onion, very thinly sliced

2 tablespoons sherry vinegar

1 ripe avocado, pitted, peeled, and thinly sliced

1 head Bibb lettuce, leaves separated

1 large tomato, thinly sliced

1 Preheat the oven to 450°F.

2 Brush the bread slices with the olive oil and bake for 6 to 7 minutes, until toasty and golden brown. Remove from the oven and rub each slice of bread with the crushed garlic.

3 Cook the bacon in a medium-size saucepan over medium-high heat until crisp. Pat dry on paper towels and set aside.

4 Mix the lobster meat, mayonnaise, chipotle pepper, Worcestershire sauce, lemon juice, and tarragon in a medium-size bowl. Season with salt and pepper to taste. Set aside. Combine the red onion and vinegar in a small bowl. Set aside.

5 To assemble the sandwiches, place two slices of bread on a cutting board. On one slice, place slices of avocado, some of the lobster mixture, some of the onion mixture, and one or two lettuce leaves. On the other slice of bread, place a thin layer of the lobster mixture, a tomato slice or two, 2 slices of bacon, and one or two lettuce leaves. Flip one side of the sandwich on top of the other, with the fillings in the middle, press firmly, and slice in half. Repeat with the remaining bread slices, and serve each person half a sandwich, with some Smoked Paprika Potato Chips (recipe follows) on the side.

Smoked Paprika Potato Chips

Vegetable oil, for frying

3 pounds russet potatoes, peeled

2 teaspoons smoked paprika
(below)

1½ tablespoons salt

1   Pour the oil into a deep fryer, or pour oil into a deep, heavy skillet to a depth of 1 inch, and heat to 330°F. Slice the potatoes very thinly, preferably with a food processor or a mandoline. If you're not frying them immediately, submerge them in cold water and set aside. Fry the potatoes until a deep golden color on both sides.

2   Combine the paprika and salt in a large mixing bowl. Toss the warm chips with the salt mixture until well coated.

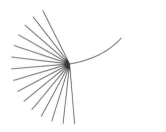

SMOKED PAPRIKA
Smoked paprika has much more depth of flavor and smokiness than regular paprika. It comes in a wide variety of levels of spiciness, so choose whichever level suits your taste.

Porcini Ravioli with Pea Pesto

Consider this a gourmet version of the picnic basket staple pasta salad. Ravioli is always a hit, and the earthy mushroom and sweet pea flavors in this version make it especially popular.

2 tablespoons butter

2 shallots, finely chopped

1 garlic clove, minced

1½ ounces dried porcini mushrooms, reconstituted (facing page) and finely chopped

2 scallions, finely chopped

1 teaspoon Worcestershire sauce

¼ cup freshly grated Parmesan cheese

Salt and freshly ground black pepper

1 recipe Pasta Dough (page 161), or 1 pound store-bought fresh pasta sheets

1 egg white, beaten

1 Melt the butter in a medium-size saucepan over medium-low heat. Add the shallots and cook until slightly golden, about 6 minutes. Add the garlic and mushrooms and cook on low heat, stirring with a wooden spoon, for 8 to 10 minutes, or until the mixture has a paste-like consistency. Remove from the heat and add the scallions, Worcestershire sauce, and Parmesan. Season with salt and pepper to taste and set aside to cool.

2 To make the ravioli, if you're using a pasta machine, roll out the dough on the thinnest setting. If using a rolling pin, dust the countertop with flour, place half the dough on the counter, and continually roll and flip it until it is as thin as possible.

3 Form the ravioli by cutting out rounds (or any shape you like) approximately 1½ inches in diameter with a cookie cutter. Work with 2 rounds at a time. Brush them both on one side with the beaten egg white. Place a heaping tablespoon of the mushroom mixture in the center of the egg-washed side of one round and press the other round on top, egg-washed side down. Seal all the edges with your fingers. Set aside on a floured baking sheet while you make the rest of the ravioli. You can make the ravioli ahead to this point and refrigerate them for 1 day or freeze them for up to 1 month.

4 When all your ravioli are made, fill a medium-size pot halfway with salted water and bring to a boil over high heat. When the water is boiling, add the ravioli. They are done when they float to the top of the water, which should take about 3 minutes. Gently toss the cooked ravioli with the Pea Pesto (recipe follows) and serve warm or at room temperature.

Pea Pesto

1 cup fresh or frozen peas, blanched

½ cup fresh mint leaves

1 tablespoon finely chopped white onion

½ teaspoon minced garlic

½ cup extra virgin olive oil

2 tablespoons chicken or vegetable broth

¼ teaspoon cayenne pepper

Salt and freshly ground black pepper

Combine the peas, mint, onion, garlic, oil, broth, cayenne, salt, and pepper in a blender and puree until you have a pourable consistency. (If it's too thick, add more broth, 1 tablespoon at a time, and puree again.)

COOKING WITH DRIED MUSHROOMS

To reconstitute dried mushrooms, soak them in hot water for 20 to 30 minutes, then drain before using.

Barbecued Chicken with Grilled Ramps and Blue Potato Salad

Try to use organic chicken in this recipe—it really does make a difference. Don't be intimidated by the long list of ingredients; it's all spices you probably have in your pantry, and the combination of flavors is perfect. You'll need to get the marinating process started at least 12 hours in advance. The Blue Potato Salad is my favorite version of potato salad, but it come with a warning: If your friends try it, they will request it all the time. The grilled ramps (also known as wild leeks) are delicious with this chicken. You may substitute scallions if you can't find ramps.

½ cup vegetable oil

1 medium-size white onion, diced

4 garlic cloves, minced

½ teaspoon ground cumin

1 teaspoon chili powder

1 teaspoon ground ginger

½ teaspoon crushed red pepper

2 whole bay leaves

2 teaspoons dried thyme

2 teaspoons dried tarragon

1 teaspoon dried basil

1 teaspoon dried oregano

Salt and freshly ground black pepper

1 cup balsamic vinegar

½ cup brown sugar

1 Heat the vegetable oil in a medium-size saucepan over high heat and cook the onion until translucent, 4 to 5 minutes. Add the garlic, cumin, chili powder, ginger, red pepper, bay leaves, thyme, tarragon, basil, and oregano. Season with salt and pepper to taste. Add the vinegar and reduce by one-third, about 5 minutes. Add the brown sugar and maple syrup, bring to a simmer, then reduce the heat to medium and simmer for another 5 minutes. Add the lime juice, lemon juice, Worcestershire sauce, tomato paste, soy sauce, and chopped tomatoes and cook on low heat for 15 minutes. Let cool, and puree in a blender until smooth.

2 Put the chickens into a baking dish, pour the marinade over the chickens, and refrigerate for at least 12 hours.

3 Prepare a hot fire on one side of a gas or charcoal grill.

1 tablespoon maple syrup

Juice of 1 lime

Juice of 1 lemon

1 tablespoon Worcestershire
sauce

2 tablespoons tomato paste

1 tablespoon soy sauce

1½ medium-size tomatoes,
chopped (about 1½ cups)

Two 3-pound whole chickens

4 Place the chickens on the grill on the side away from the fire and cover. Cook for 1 hour and 15 minutes, starting breast side up and quarter-turning the chickens every 10 minutes and basting with the marinade with each turn. Do not baste the last time you turn the chicken. When cool enough to handle, carve into serving pieces. Serve the chicken with the Grilled Ramps and Blue Potato Salad (recipes follow).

Grilled Ramps

18 ramps, washed (below)

3 tablespoons olive oil

Salt and freshly ground black
pepper

Brush the ramps with the olive oil and season them with plenty of salt and pepper. Wrap the ramps in aluminum foil and cook them on the grill over the fire for the last 12 minutes you cook the chicken.

ABOUT RAMPS

To clean ramps, rinse them in warm water, which removes dirt better than cold water. Then use a paring knife to snip off the roots at the bottom.

Blue Potato Salad

3 pounds small blue potatoes

3 garlic cloves, minced

¼ cup olive oil

1 teaspoon sherry vinegar

1 teaspoon grainy mustard

8 sprigs fennel, chopped

4 scallions, diced

Salt and freshly ground black
   pepper

1 Place the potatoes and 2 of the garlic cloves
   in a large pot filled with enough cold salted
   water to cover them. Heat on high, fully
   warming the water, but do not allow it to
   simmer or boil. Cook the potatoes in the
   warm water until a knife can pierce the
   center of a potato smoothly, approximately
   30 minutes.

2 Cool the potatoes and cut them into
   1-inch cubes. Toss with the olive oil,
   vinegar, mustard, fennel, scallions, and
   the remaining garlic clove, and season with
   salt and pepper to taste.

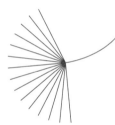

GETTING THE BLUES

Blue potatoes are also sometimes called purple potatoes. If
your grocery store doesn't carry them, use small Yukon gold,
fingerling, or red bliss potatoes instead.

Chocolate Hazelnut Tortes

Chocolate cake is a picnic staple, so we wanted to do a decadent (but not too sweet) version of it for our "picnic basket goodies" Wine Monday. Our guests absolutely loved this one. Use high-quality chocolate for this—we like Valrhona—and you'll taste the difference.

½ cup hazelnuts

18 ounces bittersweet chocolate

1½ cups (3 sticks) butter, plus
   1 teaspoon for the ramekins

1¼ cups plus 6 tablespoons
   sugar

2 tablespoons Frangelico

1¼ cups pastry flour

15 large egg whites

⅓ teaspoon salt

⅓ teaspoon cream of tartar

1 Preheat the oven to 325°F.

2 Crush the hazelnuts into a powder in a food processor; be careful that they do not become pasty.

3 Melt the chocolate and butter together in a large heatproof bowl set over simmering water. Stir 1 cup of the sugar into the melted chocolate mixture, then stir in the Frangelico. Fold in the flour and set aside to cool.

4 Place the egg whites and salt in a clean mixing bowl. Whip the egg whites with an electric mixer, adding the cream of tartar once the whites become foamy. Slowly add ¼ cup of the sugar and whip until shiny peaks form. Fold the egg whites into the chocolate mixture, gradually, then fold in half of the hazelnuts.

5 Mix together 1 teaspoon butter with the remaining 6 tablespoons sugar and the remaining hazelnuts. Coat six 8-ounce ramekins with the mixture. Divide the batter among the ramekins. Bake the tortes until the centers are firm, 30 to 35 minutes. Cool on wire racks for at least 10 minutes before serving warm or at room temperature.

L'ESPALIER FAVORITES

Once a season, we do a "favorites" menu for one of our Wine Mondays, featuring our favorite seasonal foods and wines from obscure vineyards we love. The menu can feature just about anything, and it's our chance to play around. This one is inspired by some of my personal favorite things to eat in the spring and some of L'Espalier wine director Erik Johnson's beloved wines.

MENU

& pairings

↓

 +

Warm Leeks with Goat Cheese and Spring Herb Vinaigrette

Alain Cavaillès, Brut, Blanquette de Limoux, Languedoc-Roussillon, France

Sautéed Arctic Char with Asparagus and Sorrel Sauce

2005 Domaine Laffourcade, Savennières, Loire, France

Pot-au-Feu of Poussin with Spring Vegetables and Foie Gras

2005 Domaine Parize, "Clos Les Grandes Vignes," Givry Premier Cru, Burgundy, France

Chocolate Decadence Cake with Port Sauce

2000 Rosenblum Cellars, "Carapinha," Zinfandel Port, San Francisco Bay, California

WINE ⬚ NOTES

↓

1ST PAIRING **WARM LEEKS WITH GOAT CHEESE AND SPRING HERB VINAIGRETTE**
SERVED WITH → ALAIN CAVAILLÈS, BRUT, BLANQUETTE DE LIMOUX, LANGUEDOC-ROUSSILLON, FRANCE

Blanquette de Limoux predates the Champagne region in its production of sparkling wine. (It was also the first region to use corks in its bottles.) This is a bright, apéritif style of sparkling wine—a good starter that's affordable, so you can drink as much as you want. A sparkling wine from Burgundy or California or a Sancerre would also be nice with this dish.

2ND PAIRING **SAUTÉED ARCTIC CHAR WITH ASPARAGUS AND SORREL SAUCE**
SERVED WITH → 2005 DOMAINE LAFFOURCADE, SAVENNIÈRES, LOIRE, FRANCE

This is one of the more eclectic bottles we pour for Wine Mondays. It's made from Chenin Blanc, which is an extremely malleable grape variety that can be used to make everything from bone-dry wines to dessert wines. This one is perfumey and rich enough to stand up to the asparagus and the fish. As an alternative, you could serve an unoaked Chardonnay, a dry Muscat, or a dry Viognier.

3RD PAIRING **POT-AU-FEU OF POUSSIN WITH SPRING VEGETABLES AND FOIE GRAS**
SERVED WITH → 2005 DOMAINE PARIZE, "CLOS LES GRANDES VIGNES,"
GIVRY PREMIER CRU, BURGUNDY, FRANCE

Burgundy reds are made from Pinot Noir, and this is one of wine director Erik Johnson's favorite Pinots. It has ripe fruit, rustic spice, and a nice balance that makes it great with food. Try your favorite Pinot with this dish or with just about any chicken dish.

4TH PAIRING **CHOCOLATE DECADENCE CAKE WITH PORT SAUCE**
SERVED WITH → 2000 ROSENBLUM CELLARS, "CARAPINHA," ZINFANDEL PORT,
SAN FRANCISCO BAY, CALIFORNIA

It's fun to serve port from an unexpected place. This one is made from Zinfandel grapes. It's rich and sweet, and it still tastes like Zin. Another port or Banyuls could stand in for this bottle.

Warm Leeks with Goat Cheese and Spring Herb Vinaigrette

Leeks are one of my favorite ingredients to cook with, and I wish people would cook with them more. This is a simple way to prepare leeks—but the dish is extraordinary. My favorite goat cheese to use is the Capri from Westfield Farm in Hubbardston, Massachusetts. I've been buying it since 1983. Black truffle juice is available at specialty stores and online. If you can't find it, use a tiny bit of black or white truffle oil (truffle oil can overwhelm a dish—here it should be a background flavor) or simply omit it.

12 leeks

1 garlic clove, minced

2 tablespoons champagne vinegar

6 tablespoons olive oil

1 tablespoon Dijon mustard

1 tablespoon black truffle juice

Zest and juice of 1 orange

1 tablespoon fresh thyme leaves

1 tablespoon chopped fresh chives

1 tablespoon chopped fresh tarragon

1 tablespoon chopped fresh flat-leaf parsley

1 teaspoon freshly ground black pepper

Salt

6 ounces goat cheese

1 Remove the green tops and outer layer of the leeks and slice them in half lengthwise. Place them in tepid water for 1 hour to loosen any trapped dirt.

2 While the leeks are soaking, prepare the vinaigrette. In a large bowl whisk together the garlic, vinegar, olive oil, mustard, truffle juice, orange zest and juice, thyme, chives, tarragon, parsley, and pepper. Season with salt to taste and set aside.

3 Swirl the leeks in the water to remove any remaining dirt. Steam them in a basket over boiling water for about 18 minutes, or until they are very tender to the touch. Remove the leeks from the basket and place them in the bowl with the vinaigrette. Spoon the vinaigrette over the leeks to coat them.

4 Let stand to marinate for at least 10 and up to 45 minutes before serving—make sure to serve them warm, though. To serve, place 2 leeks on each of 6 plates. Crumble the goat cheese on top of the leeks, then spoon the remaining vinaigrette over the leeks and goat cheese.

Sautéed Arctic Char with Asparagus and Sorrel Sauce

Arctic char is a relative of the salmon and the trout—in flavor and texture it falls somewhere in between. It's tender, sweet, and delicate, and one of my favorites. You can find it almost anywhere these days. The sorrel has a citrusy flavor that wakes up the palate and cuts through the richness of the protein. Look for large asparagus spears, which are sweeter.

1 cup almond flour or all-purpose flour

1 teaspoon salt

½ teaspoon freshly ground black pepper

1 teaspoon paprika

½ teaspoon dried marjoram

Six 3-ounce Arctic char fillets

2 tablespoons canola oil

1 tablespoon butter

18 asparagus spears

6 lemon wedges

Fresh sorrel leaves cut into chiffonade (facing page) for garnish

1　Combine the flour, salt, pepper, paprika, and marjoram in a wide, shallow dish. Dredge the Arctic char fillets in the flour mixture.

2　Heat a large sauté pan over medium-high heat. Add the oil and butter to the pan. When the butter is sizzling, place the fillets, skin side up, in the pan. Reduce the heat to medium and cook until golden brown, 2 to 3 minutes. Turn the fillets and cook on the other side for another 2 to 3 minutes. Remove the fillets from the pan and set them on paper towels to drain the excess fat.

3　Remove the tough bottom ends of the asparagus spears and peel them up to the tips (page 184). Steam the asparagus over boiling water for 5 minutes, or until tender.

4　Ladle a dollop of Sorrel Sauce (recipe follows) onto each of 6 plates. Place 3 steamed asparagus spears on top, then place the fish on top of the asparagus. Squeeze a lemon wedge over each piece of fish, and garnish with a sprinkle of sorrel chiffonade.

Sorrel Sauce

¼ cup dry vermouth

4 shallots, minced

2 garlic cloves, minced

1 cup white wine

1 cup vegetable or fish broth

¼ cup heavy cream

1 tablespoon fresh lemon juice

¼ teaspoon ground nutmeg

2 cups sorrel, chopped

Salt and freshly ground white
pepper

1 Combine the vermouth, shallots, and garlic in a medium-size saucepan. Simmer for 3 minutes over medium heat. Add the wine and bring to a simmer for 2 minutes. Add the broth and simmer until the liquid is reduced by one-third, about 8 minutes. Add the heavy cream and return to a simmer. Add the lemon juice and nutmeg and return to a simmer. Fold in the sorrel and cook for 1 minute.

2 Remove from the heat and puree the sauce in a blender. Season with salt and pepper to taste.

CHIFFONADE

To cut herbs such as sorrel or basil into a chiffonade, fold the leaves of the herbs in half so the stem is exposed. Use a paring knife to cut the stem out of the leaf. Then layer the leaves together and roll them into a long tube. Use a sharp chef's knife and chop across the tube so you're left with long strips reminiscent of confetti.

Pot-au-Feu of Poussin with Spring Vegetables and Foie Gras

Ah, young chicken in springtime. Also known as Cornish game hens, poussins are young spring chickens—one of my favorite things to cook and eat in this season. The foie gras here complements the leanness of the hens and brings sweetness and a nice fatty richness that will satisfy all your needs. It really makes this dish amazing, but you could leave it out if you can't find it or don't want to purchase it. You could also substitute tofu, which, interestingly, has a similar texture and degree of sweetness.

---

5 shallots, minced

¼ cup port

1 cup chicken broth

One 750-ml bottle Pinot Noir

1 *bouquet garni* (facing page)

3 whole black peppercorns

3 Cornish game hens, washed and patted dry, legs trussed (page 149)

2 leeks, washed and cut into thirds

12 carrots, peeled and cut into chunks

12 turnips, peeled and cut into chunks

1 Prepare a bouillon by combining the shallots, port, chicken broth, Pinot Noir, *bouquet garni*, and peppercorns in a large saucepan over medium heat. Bring to a simmer and cook for 5 minutes, then reduce the heat to low.

2 Submerge the game hens in the bouillon (it's safer if you do this over low heat). Turn the heat back up to medium to bring the liquid back to a simmer, then turn the heat back down to low and cook for 15 minutes.

3 Remove the game hens from the bouillon and set aside. Immediately add the leeks, carrots, turnips, potatoes, celery, and onions to the bouillon. Turn the heat up to medium-low to bring the liquid to a light simmer, then turn the heat back down to low and cook for 10 minutes. Add the foie gras to the saucepan and cook for 8 more minutes.

12 fingerling potatoes

3 celery stalks, cut into thirds

12 pearl onions

1 pound grade A foie gras

1 tablespoon minced fresh
   flat-leaf parsley

1 tablespoon fresh thyme leaves

1 tablespoon minced fresh sage

Salt and freshly ground black
   pepper

4 While the vegetables are cooking, remove the game hen meat from the bones and divide it among 6 bowls.

5 When the vegetables are cooked, remove and discard the *bouquet garni*, lift the vegetables from the bouillon with a slotted spoon, and distribute them among the bowls. Remove the foie gras and cut it into 6 pieces. Add a piece to each bowl. Sprinkle the parsley, thyme, and sage over each portion. Taste the bouillon for seasoning and add salt and pepper if desired. Ladle the bouillon over the contents of each bowl, and serve.

BOUQUET GARNI

A *bouquet garni* is a bunch of herbs tied together with butcher twine or string and used to flavor stocks and sauces, then discarded. Prepare a *bouquet garni* by using the outer layer of a trimmed leek to wrap up 2 bay leaves, 4 sprigs thyme, 1 sprig rosemary, 4 sprigs sage, and 5 parsley stems. Secure the bundle by tying butcher twine around the outer leek layer. Leave a long tail of twine so you can tie it to a pot handle for easy removal.

Chocolate Decadence Cake with Port Sauce

A chocolate cake doesn't have to be complicated to be a favorite. Sweet, deep port sauce complements this rich, chocolaty, not-too-dense dessert—which we pair with a delicious American Zinfandel port. Expect the cakes to turn out flatter than a typical cake baked in a 9-inch pan.

6 ounces bittersweet chocolate

½ cup (1 stick) butter

3 tablespoons all-purpose flour

½ cup sugar

2 tablespoons unsweetened
   cocoa powder

5 large egg whites, at room
   temperature

Pinch of salt

Pinch of cream of tartar

1 Preheat the oven to 375°F. Grease two 9-inch cake pans and line them with parchment paper.

2 Melt the chocolate with the butter in a large heatproof bowl set over a pot of simmering water.

3 In a separate bowl, sift together the flour, 6 tablespoons of the sugar, and the cocoa powder. Add the flour mixture to the melted chocolate and butter and stir to blend.

4 In another bowl, gently beat or whisk the egg whites until soft peaks form (do not overbeat or they will not incorporate easily into the chocolate mixture). While beating, slowly add the remaining 2 tablespoons sugar, the salt, and the cream of tartar to the egg whites. Carefully fold half of the egg whites into the chocolate mixture until just incorporated. Fold in the remaining half of the egg whites.

5 Divide the batter evenly between the prepared pans. Bake for 30 minutes, or until just set. Let cool for 30 minutes. Serve at room temperature with Port Sauce (recipe follows).

Port Sauce

One 750-ml bottle ruby port

⅓ cup sugar

1 Combine the port and sugar in a large saucepan over high heat. Bring to a boil and cook until the liquid is reduced by two-thirds, about 10 minutes.

2 Let cool to room temperature. You can make this sauce ahead and store it in the refrigerator for several weeks. Bring to room temperature before serving.

CHOCOLATE ACCENTS
Chocolate Decadence Cake is also delicious with fresh figs, a puree of fresh berries, or warm chocolate sauce—because you can never have too much chocolate.

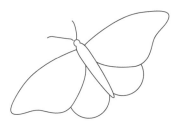

SUMMER

SOUTH AFRICA

Wines from South Africa are very good and very inexpensive. They are well made, and they offer a tremendous relative value. South African wines generally show lots of forward fruit without a lot of oak, which makes them perfect for a summer party. The ripe vegetables and fruits of summer, as well as seasonal staples like fresh-caught fish and simple grilled steaks, are natural partners for the wines of South Africa.

 SUMMER → **South Africa**

MENU

& pairings

↓

 +

PAIRINGS

Vegetable Gratin with Tomato-Saffron Coulis

1

2005 Southern Right, Sauvignon Blanc, Walker Bay

Seviche of Striped Bass with Lime-Cucumber Salsa

2

2005 Mulderbosch, Chenin Blanc, Stellenbosch

Grilled Rib-Eye Steaks with Frank's Potato Gratin

3

2001 Jardin, Cabernet Sauvignon, Stellenbosch

Sweet Corn Ice Cream with Tarragon Huckleberries

4

2005 Rudera, "Noble Late Harvest," Chenin Blanc, Stellenbosch

WINE 🍷 NOTES

↓

1ST PAIRING **VEGETABLE GRATIN WITH TOMATO-SAFFRON COULIS**
SERVED WITH → **2005 SOUTHERN RIGHT, SAUVIGNON BLANC, WALKER BAY**

California Sauvignon Blanc often has added oak; South African Sauvignon Blanc generally doesn't, which means it's fresher and vibrant, a good way to start a meal, and a nice accompaniment to a vegetable dish. You could also try another unoaked Sauvignon Blanc here.

2ND PAIRING **SEVICHE OF STRIPED BASS WITH LIME-CUCUMBER SALSA**
SERVED WITH → **2005 MULDERBOSCH, CHENIN BLANC, STELLENBOSCH**

There's a lot of Chenin Blanc in South Africa, and Mulderbosch is one of its more famous producers. This bottle has nice fruit and fresh intensity, and it's ripe but not sweet. Another dry Chenin Blanc would work nicely with this fish dish.

3RD PAIRING **GRILLED RIB-EYE STEAKS WITH FRANK'S POTATO GRATIN**
SERVED WITH → **2001 JARDIN, CABERNET SAUVIGNON, STELLENBOSCH**

We like South African Cabernet Sauvignon. It features rich fruit, like California Cabernet, but it also demonstrates an earthy restraint, like Cabernet from Bordeaux. Your favorite Cabernet Sauvignon is a natural pairing with a rib-eye steak, which just might be the ultimate piece of red meat.

4TH PAIRING **SWEET CORN ICE CREAM WITH TARRAGON HUCKLEBERRIES**
SERVED WITH → **2005 RUDERA, "NOBLE LATE HARVEST," CHENIN BLANC, STELLENBOSCH**

This is an example of a sweet Chenin Blanc—the fruit stayed on the vine until it was ready for dessert. Another sweet golden wine, such as Sauternes or Muscat, would be nice with this ice cream and fruit combo.

Vegetable Gratin with Tomato-Saffron Coulis

I have so many wonderful food memories from growing up with my grand-mother. This is a version of one summer dish she used to prepare frequently. It speaks of the garden, and it pays homage to her love of fresh vegetables.

1 large zucchini, thinly sliced
   lengthwise

1 large summer squash, thinly
   sliced lengthwise

1 large eggplant, thinly sliced
   lengthwise

2 garlic cloves, crushed

Salt and freshly ground black
   pepper

2 teaspoons dried oregano

1 teaspoon chili powder

5 tablespoons olive oil

½ cup store-bought black olive
   tapenade

½ cup store-bought pesto

8 ounces goat cheese

1 Rub the zucchini, summer squash, and eggplant with the crushed garlic and season with salt and pepper. Sprinkle with the oregano and chili powder. Set the vegetable slices in a colander to drain for 30 minutes to 1 hour, keeping each type of vegetable separate so you can layer them later.

2 Preheat the oven to 375°F. Brush the inside of a glass loaf pan with 1 tablespoon of the olive oil.

3 Heat a large sauté pan over medium-high heat. Add the remaining 4 tablespoons olive oil to the pan. When the oil is hot, sauté the zucchini, then the summer squash, and then the eggplant for about 30 seconds on each side, working in batches. Set each batch aside while you sauté the remaining vegetables.

4 Layer the sliced vegetables in the loaf pan, starting with a single layer of the zucchini. Brush some of the tapenade and pesto over the zucchini, then add a layer of summer squash. Brush more of the tapenade and pesto over the squash, then add a layer of eggplant. Brush the eggplant with tapenade and pesto and sprinkle it with goat cheese, covering the entire layer, then repeat the layers until you've used all the vegetables.

5 Bake for 20 to 25 minutes. Let cool for at least 5 minutes before slicing and serving with Tomato-Saffron Coulis (page 112).

Tomato-Saffron Coulis

2 large tomatoes

2 tablespoons white wine

½ teaspoon saffron

1 tablespoon garlic paste (below)

1 teaspoon store-bought pesto

1 teaspoon store-bought black
  olive tapenade

¼ cup extra virgin olive oil

1 teaspoon salt

5 grinds black pepper

1 teaspoon aged sherry vinegar

1 Blanch, peel (page 123), and seed the tomatoes, capturing the juice through a strainer when you seed them and reserving the juice.

2 Combine the wine and saffron in a small saucepan over medium heat. When the wine and saffron start to steam, after about 3 minutes, remove from the heat, cover, and let stand for 15 minutes.

3 Combine the reserved tomato juice, wine and saffron, garlic paste, pesto, tapenade, oil, salt, pepper, and vinegar in the bowl of a food processor and puree until smooth.

GARLIC PASTE

We use garlic paste often at L'Espalier to add deep garlic flavor to sauces, vinaigrettes, crostini, meats, and more. We prepare it confit style (cooked in oil) as follows. (You can also purchase garlic paste, but the flavor won't be quite as good.) Submerge a whole head of garlic in olive oil in a small sauce-pan. Heat it on medium heat, and when the oil starts to bubble, turn the heat down to low and cover. Cook for 20 minutes, then remove the pan from the heat and let the garlic cool in the oil. Once cool, slice the garlic head in half across the cloves, and squeeze the garlic paste out of the skins into a strainer. Use a plastic spatula to push the garlic through the strainer and into a storage container. The paste will keep for up to 5 weeks in the refrigerator.

Seviche of Striped Bass with Lime-Cucumber Salsa

I'm a fisherman, and I fish for striped bass in the summer. When I pull in a keeper (30 inches or longer), I like to fillet it right on the boat. I always keep lemons, limes, and olive oil on board so that I can prepare an easy interpretation of seviche, a dish in which the acid in the citrus juices cooks the protein of the fish quickly; with very thin slices of fish it takes just 20 seconds or so. When I'm making this at home, I use this preparation and serve the fish almost immediately after brushing it with the vinaigrette. For this dish, use the best-quality fish you can find.

Zest and juice of 1 lime

Zest and juice of 1 lemon

1 shallot, minced

1 garlic clove, minced

2 tablespoons olive oil

1 teaspoon rice wine vinegar

½ teaspoon soy sauce

½ teaspoon honey

1 teaspoon chopped fresh
  cilantro

1 teaspoon chopped fresh chives

1 teaspoon chopped fresh
  flat-leaf parsley

¼ teaspoon cayenne pepper

2 teaspoons minced fresh ginger

One 5-ounce skinless striped
  bass fillet

1 Combine the lime and lemon zests and juices, shallot, garlic, olive oil, vinegar, soy sauce, honey, cilantro, chives, parsley, cayenne, and ginger in a food processor and blend until you have a uniform consistency.

2 Cut the bass into ¼-inch-thick strips and divide them evenly among 6 chilled plates (3 to 4 pieces per plate). Liberally brush the lemon-lime mixture over the fish.

3 Spoon Lime-Cucumber Salsa (page 114) in a thick line across the center of each plate and serve at once.

1 large cucumber, peeled,
  seeded, and diced

Juice of 1 lime

1 tablespoon chopped fresh
  cilantro

2 tablespoons diced red onion

Salt and freshly ground black
  pepper

Combine the cucumber, lime juice, cilantro, onion, salt, and pepper in a medium-size bowl and mix well.

SASSY SALSA

Adding diced tomato, fresh or roasted tomatillo, peach, nectarine, or melon to this salsa gives it a delicious new flavor.

Grilled Rib-Eye Steaks with Frank's Potato Gratin

Rib-eye is my favorite cut of steak because it has the most flavor. My kids love it grilled this way. Anyone who loves to grill but gets scared of cookbook recipes can handle this one easily. The steak goes well with my potato gratin, also an easy dish to master. People tend to think of potato gratin as containing cheese— mine is just cream and potatoes, flavored with leeks, nutmeg, salt, and pepper.

3 tablespoons butter, at room temperature

2 garlic cloves, crushed

1 tablespoon minced fresh rosemary

Salt and freshly ground black pepper

6 rib-eye steaks, washed and patted dry

1 tablespoon Worcestershire sauce

1 Combine the butter, garlic, rosemary, salt, and pepper and rub the mixture all over the steaks. Sprinkle the Worcestershire sauce on each steak. Let stand for 30 minutes.

2 Prepare a hot fire in a charcoal or gas grill.

3 Cook the steaks on the grill for 3½ minutes on each side for medium-rare. Serve with Frank's Potato Gratin (page 116).

Frank's Potato Gratin

1 tablespoon olive oil

1 garlic clove, crushed

4 medium-size potatoes, peeled
and very thinly sliced

1 leek, sliced into thin rounds
and washed

1 tablespoon fresh thyme leaves

½ teaspoon ground nutmeg

Salt and freshly ground black
pepper

1¼ cups heavy cream

1 Preheat the oven to 400°F.

2 Brush the oil all over the inside of a 9-inch pie plate. Rub the garlic all over the pie plate. Line the pie plate with a layer of potatoes, overlapping them in a fan pattern. Distribute some sliced leeks over the potatoes and season with some of the thyme, nutmeg, salt, and pepper. Drizzle with some of the cream. Repeat this layering pattern, adding cream to each layer.

3 When you have layered all the ingredients, press down firmly on the potatoes. The cream should reach the top layer; if it doesn't, add enough cream to reach the top.

4 Cover the pie plate with aluminum foil or a lid. Bake for 15 minutes, or until the dish starts to simmer. Uncover and reduce the oven temperature to 375°F. Bake for an additional 30 minutes, or until golden brown. Remove from the oven and let cool for 10 minutes. You can make this dish ahead of time and reheat it in the oven at 350°F for 20 minutes.

Sweet Corn Ice Cream
with Tarragon Huckleberries

I love sweet corn in any course, and it's a treat to have it for dessert. It tastes incredible with fruits that are in season at the same time as the corn. Look for huckleberries at farmers' markets, but if you can't find them, use blueberries.

2 ears corn

2½ cups milk

2 cups heavy cream

½ teaspoon fresh lemon juice

½ teaspoon pure vanilla extract

¾ cup sugar

9 large egg yolks

Pinch of salt

1 Remove the kernels from the cobs and cut the cobs into ½-inch-thick slices. Combine the kernels, sliced cobs, milk, cream, lemon juice, and vanilla in a large nonreactive saucepan and simmer gently for 1 hour over low heat. Remove from the heat and let sit for another hour to infuse. Strain the liquid and discard the cobs, reserving the corn and the liquid.

2 Place the corn kernels in a blender with 1 cup of the milk mixture and puree. Strain the puree back into the remaining milk mixture, add ½ cup of the sugar, and heat in the saucepan over low heat.

3 Beat the egg yolks in an electric mixer with the remaining ¼ cup sugar until thick and pale yellow. Gradually pour about one-third of the hot milk mixture into the whipped eggs to temper them. Pour the egg mixture into the remaining milk mixture and cook over low heat, stirring constantly, until the mixture is thick enough to coat the back of a spoon. An instant-read thermometer dipped into the mixture should read 160°F.

(continued)

4 Remove the pan from the heat, stir in the salt, and transfer the mixture to another bowl that you can cool in an ice bath (page 21). Place the bowl in the ice bath, stir until cool, then remove from the ice bath, cover, and refrigerate overnight.

5 Freeze the mixture in an ice cream maker according to the manufacturer's instructions. Serve with Tarragon Huckleberries (recipe follows).

Tarragon Huckleberries

3 cups huckleberries, washed (below) and stems removed

⅓ cup sugar

½ cup fresh orange juice

1 tablespoon fresh tarragon

1 Combine 1 cup of the huckleberries with the sugar and orange juice in a small heatproof mixing bowl. Heat over a pot of gently simmering water for about 1 hour, stirring occasionally. Remove from the heat, let cool slightly, then transfer to a blender and add the tarragon. Blend, then pour through a strainer back into the mixing bowl. Heat the puree again over the simmering water until hot.

2 Put the remaining 2 cups huckleberries in a large bowl and pour the heated puree over them. Serve immediately, or cover and refrigerate for up to 2 days. Reheat gently before serving.

WASHING WILD BERRIES

Put the berries in a bowl and fill it with cold water. The stems and leaves will float to the top. Skim them off the surface. Lift the berries out of the water and place them in a colander to drain.

FRENCH ABCs

It's fun to tour the wine regions of France from your own table like this: starting in Alsace, moving on to Burgundy and Bordeaux, and finishing in Champagne. When we do a French ABCs wine dinner at L'Espalier, we always try to start with A, move on to the Bs, and conclude with C—and to present some unexpected wines from these regions. It can be a challenge depending on what food we're serving, but it's fun to play around. If someone at your dinner has been to one or all of these regions, ask them to share memories of their travels. This summer version of the ABCs is a perfect way to celebrate Bastille Day, which is July 14.

MENU

& pairings
↓

 +

PAIRINGS

**Heirloom Tomato Soup
with Succotash**

1

**2004 Domaine Valentin Zusslin,
"Pinot d'Alsace Vieilles Vignes,"
Sylvaner, Alsace**

**Butter and Herb–Poached
Maine Lobster with Cucumber,
Avocado, and Nasturtium Salad**

2

**2004 Jean-Marc Brocard,
Sauvignon de Saint Bris,
Burgundy**

**Roasted Duck with
Ginger and Plums**

3

**2001 Château
Villa Bel-Air,
Graves, Bordeaux**

**Nick's Wild Mint Ice Cream
with Warm Berries**

4

**Veuve Clicquot Ponsardin,
Demi-Sec, Champagne**

WINE 🍾 NOTES

↓

1ST PAIRING **HEIRLOOM TOMATO SOUP WITH SUCCOTASH**
SERVED WITH → 2004 DOMAINE VALENTIN ZUSSLIN, "PINOT D'ALSACE VIEILLES VIGNES," SYLVANER, ALSACE

Alsace is generally associated with Riesling, Gewürztraminer, and Pinot Gris. But the region also grows Sylvaner, which is sometimes dismissed as an unimportant varietal. With enough love, though, it can develop a rich and concentrated flavor that stands up to the flavor of fresh tomato. An Alsace Pinot Gris would also be nice here.

2ND PAIRING **BUTTER AND HERB–POACHED MAINE LOBSTER WITH CUCUMBER, AVOCADO, AND NASTURTIUM SALAD**
SERVED WITH → 2004 JEAN-MARC BROCARD, SAUVIGNON DE SAINT BRIS, BURGUNDY

Bring together lobster, avocado, and butter and you have a rich, decadent dish. So for your wine, you want something bright and acidic to cut through all that. This is a Sauvignon Blanc from the only part of Burgundy that grows Sauvignon Blanc. A crisp white such as Chablis or a dry Champagne are other good choices.

3RD PAIRING **ROASTED DUCK WITH GINGER AND PLUMS**
SERVED WITH → 2001 CHÂTEAU VILLA BEL-AIR, GRAVES, BORDEAUX

Merlot is the main component of this soft, fruit-forward red wine from the south of Bordeaux. Alternatively, pair a Pinot Noir or a California Merlot with this dish.

4TH PAIRING **NICK'S WILD MINT ICE CREAM WITH WARM BERRIES**
SERVED WITH → VEUVE CLICQUOT PONSARDIN, DEMI-SEC, CHAMPAGNE

As promised, here's something from Champagne to finish: a sweet-style champagne. You could also serve a sweet-style prosecco, or a non-sparkling light, sweet dessert wine here.

Heirloom Tomato Soup with Succotash

Serve this soup at room temperature, not chilled, so the tomato flavor can really shine. This dish is incredibly simple, and it lets the tomatoes speak for themselves. I add a tiny bit of sherry vinegar, because I think it brings out the flavor of the tomatoes, and that's about it. You could use your favorite tomatoes from your garden, or the tomatoes from your local farm stand or farmers' market. Whatever you do, use excellent, local tomatoes in season. Midwinter grocery store tomatoes simply will not do.

3 pounds ripe tomatoes (preferably a mix of heirloom varieties)

1 tablespoon sherry vinegar

2 teaspoons salt, or to taste

2 teaspoons freshly ground black pepper, or to taste

2 tablespoons extra virgin olive oil

1 Blanch, peel (below), and seed the tomatoes, straining the seeds in order to capture as much juice as possible.

2 Puree the tomatoes and their juice in a food processor until smooth. Add the vinegar, salt, and pepper and blend until well incorporated. Serve in bowls over Succotash (page 124), and drizzle each bowl with a teaspoon of olive oil.

PEELING TOMATOES

To remove the skins from tomatoes, core them and cut a small X on one end. Prepare a small bowl of ice water. Bring some water to a boil in a small saucepan and carefully place the tomatoes in the boiling water. After 10 seconds, remove with a slotted spoon and immediately place in the ice water until they are completely cool. Remove the tomatoes from the water, and the skins should slip off easily.

Succotash

2 ears corn, with their husks

1 bunch fresh basil leaves (about 2 loosely packed cups)

3 garlic cloves

1 teaspoon salt

1 teaspoon freshly ground black pepper

3 teaspoons olive oil

½ cup fresh or frozen lima beans, blanched

½ cup fresh or frozen fava beans, blanched

½ cup green beans, blanched and sliced into ½-inch pieces

½ cup diced red onion

One 6-ounce ball buffalo mozzarella or regular fresh mozzarella cheese, cut into 1-inch strips

1 Preheat the oven to 400°F.

2 Bake the corn (with the husks on) for 25 minutes.

3 While the corn is baking, make a pesto by combining the basil, garlic, salt, and pepper in the bowl of a food processor. While blending, slowly add the olive oil, pureeing until smooth.

4 Let the corn cool, then remove the husks and cut the kernels off the cobs. Combine the corn, lima beans, fava beans, green beans, onion, and mozzarella and toss with the pesto mixture.

Butter and Herb–Poached Maine Lobster with Cucumber, Avocado, and Nasturtium Salad

At L'Espalier we use day-boat Maine lobster, which means we get the lobster the same day it's taken out of the water. Our cultured butter comes from Vermont Butter & Cheese Company, and it is readily available in better supermarkets. Use the best, freshest lobster and butter you can find and this dish will be not just special but unforgettable. Use fresh herbs, and leave them whole for poaching. I've been making this dish since I ate at Alain Chapel in Burgundy in 1989. He had a lobster dish with herbs on his menu, and it moved me. When I came back to Boston I worked on perfecting my own version. This is it.

Three 1¼-pound live hard-shell lobsters

1 cup (2 sticks) butter

1 dried chipotle chile, chopped

1 tablespoon fresh tarragon leaves

1 tablespoon fresh rosemary leaves

1 tablespoon fresh flat-leaf parsley leaves

1 tablespoon chopped fresh chives

1 teaspoon fresh lemon thyme leaves or regular thyme leaves

1 teaspoon fresh oregano leaves

2 teaspoons salt, plus more for serving

1 Place a large pot with 2 inches of water over high heat. When the water is just simmering, plunge the lobsters headfirst into the water and cover. Reduce the heat to medium-high and cook for 6 minutes. Remove the lobsters from the pot and let cool.

2 Remove the lobster meat from the shells, claws, knuckles, and tail and set aside.

3 In a small saucepan, melt the butter over low heat and add the chipotle, tarragon, rosemary, parsley, chives, thyme, oregano, and salt. Cook on low heat, never allowing the butter to simmer, for 4 minutes. Add the lobster meat and poach for 5 minutes. Remove the tails from the butter and slice them in half lengthwise. Distribute the lobster meat evenly on a platter, pour the butter over the lobster, and season with a sprinkle of salt. Serve with Cucumber, Avocado, and Nasturtium Salad (page 126).

Cucumber, Avocado, and Nasturtium Salad

1 large cucumber

1 avocado

10 nasturtium flowers (below), rinsed and chopped

1 tablespoon fresh orange juice

1 tablespoon fresh yuzu juice (below)

1 tablespoon minced shallot

Salt and freshly ground black pepper

1 Peel and thinly slice the cucumber. Remove the pit and skin from the avocado and dice the flesh. Combine the cucumber, avocado, and nasturtium flowers in a medium-size bowl and toss gently.

2 Whisk together the orange juice, yuzu juice, and shallot. Season with salt and pepper to taste. Pour over the salad and toss gently to combine.

EDIBLE BLOSSOMS

Look for colorful nasturtium flowers in the produce section of large supermarkets or at farmers' markets.

YUZU

Yuzu is an Asian citrus fruit that resembles a small, somewhat ugly grapefruit. It's available at many better grocery stores and produce shops, as well as Japanese and Korean markets. If you can't find yuzu, substitute grapefruit juice, or just use 2 tablespoons fresh orange juice.

Roasted Duck with Ginger and Plums

Duck was my favorite food when I was a little boy. When we went out to dinner when I was as young as 4 or 5, I always ordered duck à l'orange. It's still a favorite of mine, and my children love it now. So of course I had to present a duck recipe for you and your family to try.

¼ cup plus 1 tablespoon soy sauce

¾ cup fresh orange juice

2 tablespoons honey

4 tablespoons chopped fresh ginger

1 teaspoon Chinese five-spice powder

4 garlic cloves, minced

1 teaspoon crushed red pepper

2 whole ducks (about 3 pounds each)

6 ripe plums

1 cup red wine

¼ cup port

1 star anise pod

1 cinnamon stick

4 whole peppercorns

1 Make a marinade by combining ¼ cup of the soy sauce, ¼ cup of the orange juice, the honey, 3 tablespoons of the ginger, the five-spice powder, garlic, and red pepper. Place the ducks in a large plastic bag, pour in the marinade, and tie tightly, pressing out as much air as possible. (Or you may divide the ducks and marinade between two large zipper-top plastic bags.) Refrigerate overnight. Remove from the refrigerator 1 hour before cooking.

2 Preheat the oven to 400°F.

3 Cut the plums in half, remove the pits, and place the plums, cut side down, in a baking dish. Add the red wine, port, the remaining ½ cup orange juice, the remaining 1 tablespoon soy sauce, the remaining 1 tablespoon ginger, the star anise, cinnamon stick, and peppercorns to the dish. Bake for 20 minutes, or until the skin starts pulling off the plums. Remove from the oven and remove the skins from the plums. Reserve the plums and the liquid from the pan.

(continued)

4   Remove the ducks from the marinade and discard marinade. Prick the skin of the ducks all over with a fork. Place a steamer rack and 1 inch of water in a large pot over high heat. When the water is boiling, place the ducks on the rack and cover. Steam for 30 minutes.

5   Remove the ducks from the rack and place them in a roasting pan. Pour the plums and the plums' cooking liquid over the ducks. Reduce the oven temperature to 350°F and roast the ducks for 1 hour and 20 minutes, basting every 20 minutes (add water to the pan if needed for basting).

6   Remove the ducks from the oven and let stand for 15 minutes. Place the plums on a serving platter, strain the remaining liquid, skim off the fat, and adjust the seasoning as desired. Carve the duck meat off the bone and serve it on a platter with the plums, accompanied by the sauce.

Nick's Wild Mint Ice Cream with Warm Berries

In the summer, pairing fresh warm berries with cold ice cream makes for an unbeatable dessert. It's simple, not stuffy or formal, and tastes amazing. We make this ice cream with wild mint brought to us by L'Espalier sommelier Nick Tranquillo, who actually came to us through Wine Mondays. Nick was a young research assistant at Harvard University, and he loved food and wine but didn't have much disposable income to spend on fancy dining. He read about Wine Mondays soon after we started the program in 2002, and decided he could afford the reasonable price. He came week after week and got to know wine director Erik Johnson, and started asking more and more questions and studying wine. Soon he became part of our staff. In addition to being a walking food and wine encyclopedia, it turns out he knows where to find outstanding wild mint.

---

2 cups heavy cream

2¼ cups milk

2 cups spearmint leaves

2 large eggs

1 large egg yolk

½ cup plus 2 tablespoons sugar

1 Combine the cream, milk, and spearmint in a medium-size saucepan. Bring to a simmer over low heat and cook for 20 minutes. Strain through a fine-mesh sieve into a bowl and discard the mint.

2 In a separate bowl, whisk together the eggs, egg yolk, and 2 tablespoons of the sugar. Slowly pour one-half of the hot milk mixture into the egg mixture to temper the eggs, being careful not to pour too quickly or you may cook the eggs.

3 Pour the remaining milk mixture back into the saucepan and blend in the tempered egg-milk mixture. Heat over medium heat, stirring constantly with a rubber spatula, until the liquid is thick enough to coat the back of a spoon. An instant-read

(continued)

thermometer dipped into the liquid should read 160°F. Remove from the heat and strain into a large bowl that you can set into an ice bath (page 21). Once cool, cover the bowl and refrigerate overnight.

4 Remove from the refrigerator and freeze in an ice cream maker according to the manufacturer's instructions. Serve with Warm Berries (recipe follows). It's also terrific with hot fudge sauce.

Warm Berries

½ cup sugar

3 tablespoons water

1 tablespoon butter

½ teaspoon fresh lemon juice

2 cups mixed berries, washed (page 118)

1 Combine the sugar and water in a small sauté pan. Slowly dissolve the sugar over low heat. Once the sugar has dissolved, add the butter and lemon juice.

2 Add the berries and sauté very briefly (about 10 seconds). Remove from the heat and transfer to a bowl. Serve warm.

SUMMER SIPPERS

Our wine cravings tend to change with the seasons, and in summer we love lighter wines: crisp, dry sparklers, Sauvignon Blanc with plenty of mineral qualities, and soft reds as opposed to heavy, full-bodied selections. Our food cravings change, too. We don't want heavy, cheesy comfort food but instead want to sample more delicate bites and fresh flavors. This menu celebrates some of our favorite wines for summer, and the foods that go well with them.

MENU

& pairings

↓

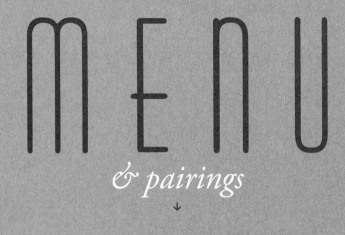

 +

PAIRINGS

Vidalia Onion, Cèpe, and Arugula Tarts

1

Louis Bouillot, "Grande Réserve," Brut, Crémant de Bourgogne, Burgundy, France

Skillet-Roasted Sea Bass with Watermelon Broth

2

2003 Jean-Marc Brocard, Sauvignon de Saint-Bris, Burgundy, France

L'Espalier's Fried Chicken and Honey Biscuits

3

2001 Brucher, Pinot Noir, Santa Barbara County, California

Blueberries with Mascarpone Sabayon

4

2003 Coturri, "Testa Vineyards," Carignane, Mendocino County, California

WINE 🍾 NOTES

↓

1ST PAIRING **VIDALIA ONION, CÈPE, AND ARUGULA TARTS**
SERVED WITH → **LOUIS BOUILLOT, "GRANDE RÉSERVE," BRUT, CRÉMANT DE BOURGOGNE, BURGUNDY, FRANCE**
This sparkling wine is made with the same grape varieties as Champagne, but it has more crispness and acidity, which means it's refreshing to sip and cuts through the richness of the pastry element in this dish. Or you could try another dry sparkling wine—always fun to sip on a summer evening.

2ND PAIRING **SKILLET-ROASTED SEA BASS WITH WATERMELON BROTH**
SERVED WITH → **2003 JEAN-MARC BROCARD, SAUVIGNON DE SAINT-BRIS, BURGUNDY, FRANCE**
This wine comes from the only place in Burgundy that produces Sauvignon Blanc. It's near Chablis, and the soil is rich in minerals. A Chablis or a Sauvignon Blanc with plenty of minerality is a good choice here.

3RD PAIRING **L'ESPALIER'S FRIED CHICKEN AND HONEY BISCUITS**
SERVED WITH → **2001 BRUCHER, PINOT NOIR, SANTA BARBARA COUNTY, CALIFORNIA**
We love this chicken accompanied by Pinot Noir. This California Pinot isn't as ripe as some Pinots from Burgundy. Try an early-harvest Pinot Noir (such as most of those from Southern California) with this dish.

4TH PAIRING **BLUEBERRIES WITH MASCARPONE SABAYON**
SERVED WITH → **2003 COTURRI, "TESTA VINEYARDS," CARIGNANE, MENDOCINO COUNTY, CALIFORNIA**
Coturri has been making organic wines in small batches for decades. This one has the fruit-forward flavor of blueberries. You could choose another fruity, jammy red here, such as a Zinfandel or a red dessert wine.

Vidalia Onion, Cèpe, and Arugula Tarts

Cèpes, the mushrooms known as porcini in Italy, are wonderfully flavorful, with a nutty earthiness that goes well with the sweetness of caramelized Vidalia onions and aromatic arugula. If you can't find fresh cèpes, use a mix of earthy wild mushrooms or dried cèpes.

1 tablespoon olive oil

2 tablespoons butter

4 medium-size Vidalia onions, thickly sliced

3 garlic cloves, minced

4 ounces fresh cèpes, or ¾ ounce dried, reconstituted cèpes (page 91), thinly sliced

1 tablespoon fresh thyme leaves

¼ cup sherry

¼ cup freshly grated Parmigiano-Reggiano cheese, plus extra for sprinkling

Juice and zest of 1 lemon

Pinch of ground nutmeg

1 tablespoon balsamic vinegar

4 ounces arugula

Salt and freshly ground black pepper

10 sprigs fresh flat-leaf parsley, finely minced

Three 8-inch puff pastry sheets

1 large egg, lightly beaten

1 Preheat the oven to 400°F.

2 Heat the oil and butter in a medium-size saucepan over medium-low heat. Add the onions and turn the heat to medium-high, then cook until they begin to caramelize and turn brown, 6 to 8 minutes. Add the garlic and stir for 10 seconds, then add the cèpes and cook for 3 minutes.

3 Add the thyme, sherry, cheese, lemon juice and zest, and nutmeg. Cook for 2 minutes, then add the vinegar and remove from the heat. Place the arugula in a medium-size bowl and pour the mixture over it. Season with salt and pepper and add the parsley. Stir to combine.

4 Place the puff pastry sheets on baking sheets (there is no need to roll them out). Pierce the pastry sheets with the tines of a fork, then brush the tops with the beaten egg. Parbake the puff pastry for 13 minutes.

5 Remove from the oven and distribute the filling evenly over the pastry sheets. Sprinkle a bit of cheese and a dash of black pepper over the top. Bake for 6 minutes. Remove from the oven, let cool, and serve at room temperature.

Skillet-Roasted Sea Bass
with Watermelon Broth

This recipe combines one of my favorite kinds of seafood with one of summer's sweetest flavors—watermelon—tempered with white wine and Lillet Blanc, a French apéritif. It's light and refreshing, and also intensely flavorful.

FOR THE BASS:

Six 5-ounce sea bass steaks

1 tablespoon store-bought basil pesto

1 tablespoon olive oil

1 lemon, sliced

1 orange, sliced

4 bay leaves

Salt and freshly ground black pepper

2 tablespoons grapeseed or vegetable oil

1 To make the bass, place the bass steaks in a baking dish. Combine the pesto, olive oil, lemon slices, orange slices, and bay leaves in a small bowl and pack the marinade ingredients around the bass steaks. Cover and refrigerate for 2 hours.

2 Preheat the oven to 450°F.

3 Salt a large cast-iron skillet over high heat with 3 pinches of salt. Add the grapeseed oil.

4 Remove the steaks from the marinade and sprinkle them with salt and pepper. Sear the steaks, skin side down, until brown, about 4 minutes. Transfer the skillet to the oven and bake for 8 to 10 minutes (depending on the thickness of the steaks), until the fish is firm to the touch.

(continued)

FOR THE BROTH:

1 tablespoon olive oil

2 shallots, chopped

3 garlic cloves, minced

1 tablespoon minced fresh
 tarragon

1 tablespoon minced fresh
 cilantro

1½ cups dry vermouth

1 cup Lillet Blanc

1½ cups white wine (such as
 Sauvignon Blanc)

1 quart watermelon juice (below)

Salt and freshly ground black
 pepper

Fresh lemon juice

5 To make the broth, heat the olive oil in a
large stockpot over medium heat. Sauté
the shallots and garlic in the oil for about 3
minutes. Add the tarragon and cilantro and
stir for 5 seconds.

6 Add the vermouth and Lillet Blanc and
cook for 3 minutes. Add the white wine and
reduce the liquid by half. Add the watermelon juice and bring to a simmer. Skim off
and discard any foam that rises to the top.

7 Add salt, pepper, and lemon juice to taste,
then place the bass in shallow soup dishes
and ladle the broth around them.

WATERMELON JUICE

For the watermelon juice, put chunks of watermelon through a
food mill or puree in a blender. Strain through a fine-mesh sieve
to extract the juice and remove the solids.

L'Espalier's Fried Chicken and Honey Biscuits

This simple recipe makes for the tastiest fried chicken ever. Use all organic ingredients if you can—but organic chicken is definitely key. You can really taste the chicken, so it should be the best you can find. The only trick to this recipe is that you need to start a day in advance so the chicken has time to marinate in the buttermilk and citrus zests.

1 quart buttermilk

Zest of 1 lemon

Zest of 1 orange

One 3- to 4-pound whole chicken (preferably organic), cut into pieces

2 cups cornmeal

2 tablespoons dried oregano

2 tablespoons smoked paprika

Salt and freshly ground black pepper

Vegetable oil for frying

1   Combine the buttermilk and lemon and orange zests in a large bowl and then submerge the chicken pieces in the mixture. Cover and refrigerate overnight.

2   Combine the cornmeal, oregano, and paprika in a flat pan or shallow bowl and sprinkle with salt and pepper.

3   Pour the oil into a deep fryer, or pour oil into a deep, heavy skillet to a depth of ¼ inch, and heat to 340°F.

4   Remove the chicken from the buttermilk, dredge the chicken pieces in the cornmeal mixture, and then fry them, being careful not to crowd them in the skillet. Using tongs, turn the chicken pieces over after 7 minutes and continue cooking until both sides are golden brown, another 6 or 7 minutes. Drain on paper towels until ready to serve with Honey Biscuits (page 138).

Honey Biscuits

2 cups all-purpose flour

1 tablespoon baking powder

1 teaspoon salt

6 tablespoons cold butter

¾ cup heavy cream

Zest of 1 lemon

2 tablespoons honey

1 tablespoon poppy seeds

1 Preheat the oven to 425°F. Lightly grease a baking sheet.

2 In a large bowl, sift together the flour, baking powder, and salt. Cut 5 table-spoons of the butter into bits and, with your fingertips or a pastry blender, blend it into the flour mixture until the mixture resembles coarse meal.

3 Add the cream, lemon zest, honey, and poppy seeds and stir with a fork until just combined.

4 Transfer the mixture to a lightly floured surface and gently knead it about 3 times, until it just forms a dough. Pat the dough into a round about 6½ inches in diameter and ½ inch thick.

5 Use a 2½-inch round cutter to cut out biscuits; arrange them about 1 inch apart on the baking sheet. Gather and pat out the scraps and cut out more biscuits.

6 Melt the remaining 1 tablespoon butter and lightly brush it onto the biscuits. Bake the biscuits in the middle of the oven until pale golden and cooked through, about 20 minutes.

Blueberries with Mascarpone Sabayon

Sabayon is a delicious custard-like sauce (the French version of the Italian zabaglione), and in this version the mascarpone makes it incredibly creamy and a little decadent. Pouring it over fruit makes a simple, just-rich-enough dessert. I love it with fresh, local blueberries in season, and it's also wonderful with strawberries or raspberries.

2½ cups light cream

1 cup sugar

3 large egg yolks

2½ cups mascarpone cheese

⅔ cup amontillado sherry

2 pints blueberries, washed
  (page 118)

1 Heat the cream gently in a medium-size saucepan over low heat until it's just heated through.

2 In a medium-size bowl, beat together the sugar and egg yolks. Pour the cream slowly into the sugar mixture, whisking and being careful not to cook the eggs. Return the mixture to the pan and heat it until an instant-read thermometer dipped into it registers 180°F. Remove the pan from the heat and let the mixture cool to 110°F.

3 Put the mascarpone in a medium-size bowl, pour the cream mixture over it, and whisk until thoroughly combined. Thin the sabayon by whisking in the sherry. To serve, divide the blueberries among 6 dessert bowls and pour the sabayon over them.

LIKE, WOW . . . TOTALLY ORGANIC

Organic wine is the wave of the future. Of course, many vineyards have been growing grapes organically for decades, or even centuries. This practice develops better fruit and better intensity of flavor from the grape and so creates better wine. You'll see more and more of this kind of wine on the shelves of your favorite wine store. So many European vineyards have been organic forever, and they don't feel the need to talk about it or advertise it—they just make better wines because of it. And, of course, I love organic ingredients, too. At L'Espalier, we buy from as many small producers as possible that are 100 percent organic. We've always done that, because we think the product is superior. We don't tout it much; it's just what we do. Pairing a meal filled with organic ingredients with organically grown wines just makes sense.

SUMMER → Like, Wow... Totally Organic

menu

& pairings

↓

 +

PAIRINGS

Open-Faced Tomato-Cheddar Sandwiches with Poached Eggs	**1**	**2001 Domaine Valentin Zusslin, "Pfingstberg," Grand Cru, Riesling, Alsace, France**
Crab-Corn Fritters with Cucumber-Watercress Salad	**2**	**2004 Alain Guillot, Mâcon Cruzille, Burgundy, France**
Roasted Capon and Endive	**3**	**2003 Domaine les Fouques, Côtes de Provence, France**
Watermelon Sorbet with Fresh Basil	**4**	**2005 Traginer, Banyuls Blanc, Roussillon, France**

WINE 🍷 NOTES

↓

1ST PAIRING **OPEN-FACED TOMATO-CHEDDAR SANDWICHES WITH POACHED EGGS**
SERVED WITH → 2001 DOMAINE VALENTIN ZUSSLIN, "PFINGSTBERG," GRAND CRU, RIESLING, ALSACE, FRANCE

People say eggs are difficult to pair with wine, but they don't have to be. Stay away from oaky, buttery Chardonnay and opt for a wine that's dry but with some richness, like this biodynamic (even more rigorous than organic) Riesling—or an Austrian Riesling or a Grüner Veltliner.

2ND PAIRING **CRAB-CORN FRITTERS WITH CUCUMBER-WATERCRESS SALAD**
SERVED WITH → 2004 ALAIN GUILLOT, MÂCON CRUZILLE, BURGUNDY, FRANCE

An organic Chardonnay from the southern part of Burgundy, this bottle has plenty of richness but not much oak. Any not-too-oaky Chardonnay or an Albariño from Spain would be lovely with these fritters.

3RD PAIRING **ROASTED CAPON AND ENDIVE**
SERVED WITH → 2003 DOMAINE LES FOUQUES, CÔTES DE PROVENCE, FRANCE

Made mostly from Grenache and Syrah grapes, this biodynamic red is grown on an estate that also produces organic chicken and eggs for Michelin-starred restaurants in the area. So we thought it was a good choice for this poultry dish. Also good would be a flavorful red like a Grenache, a Côtes du Rhône, or a richer Pinot Noir (as you know by now, we do love chicken with Pinot).

4TH PAIRING **WATERMELON SORBET WITH FRESH BASIL**
SERVED WITH → 2005 TRAGINER, BANYULS BLANC, ROUSSILLON, FRANCE

Banyuls is most often red, but there is occasionally white Banyuls made from Grenache Blanc or Grenache Gris grapes. This wine is delicious and not overly sweet, with hints of white peach and apricot. Moscato d'Asti pairs well with this sorbet, too.

Open-Faced Tomato-Cheddar Sandwiches with Poached Eggs

This is an amazing open-faced grilled cheese sandwich. Use the freshest organic local eggs that you can possibly find, and try to use two different kinds of heirloom tomatoes. For the cheese, I love to use 1-year-aged Grafton cheddar.

1 garlic clove, crushed

Six 1½-inch-thick slices sourdough bread

2 tablespoons olive oil

2 large tomatoes, sliced

6 ounces cheddar cheese, very thinly sliced

1 tablespoon salt, plus more for seasoning the sandwiches

Freshly ground black pepper

1 tablespoon balsamic vinegar

6 large eggs

1 Preheat the oven to 400°F.

2 Rub the garlic onto the bread slices, then brush the bread with the oil and arrange it on a large baking sheet. Toast the bread in the oven for 5 minutes.

3 Remove the baking sheet from the oven and layer the tomato slices, then the cheese slices, on the bread, distributing the tomatoes and cheese evenly among the bread slices. Season with salt and pepper, then return the baking sheet to the oven and toast the sandwiches for another 5 minutes.

4 Meanwhile, bring 2 quarts of water to a boil with 1 tablespoon salt and the vinegar in a medium-size saucepan over high heat. When the water is boiling, crack the eggs into the pot. When the water returns to a simmer, reduce the heat to medium. Cook the eggs for 5 minutes, remove with a slotted spoon, and transfer them to the tops of the tomato-cheddar sandwiches. Spoon Egg Yolk–Caper Sauce (recipe follows) over each sandwich and serve hot.

Egg Yolk–Caper Sauce

1 large egg yolk

2 tablespoons balsamic vinegar

1 garlic clove, minced

1 tablespoon fresh orange juice

2 teaspoons Dijon mustard

2 tablespoons capers, rinsed and dried

½ teaspoon salt, or to taste

¼ teaspoon freshly ground black pepper, or to taste

6 tablespoons olive oil

1 tablespoon chopped fresh chives

Whisk together the egg yolk, vinegar, garlic, orange juice, mustard, capers, salt, and pepper until well blended. Slowly whisk in the olive oil until emulsified. Fold in the chives and serve immediately.

Note: This sauce contains raw egg, so it is best not to serve it to anyone with a compromised immune system.

Crab-Corn Fritters with Cucumber-Watercress Salad

These fritters are addictive on their own and great to serve as hors d'oeuvres at a summer cocktail party. If you pair them with the crisp cucumber-watercress salad, you have an incredibly fresh and flavorful summer course. Use fresh corn kernels if you can, as it makes a big difference in the flavor.

2 cups cooked corn kernels

4 large eggs, separated

½ cup buttermilk

1 cup all-purpose flour

2 teaspoons salt

1½ teaspoons baking powder

¼ teaspoon cayenne pepper

¼ pound fresh lump crabmeat, picked over

¼ cup vegetable oil

1 Combine the corn, egg yolks, and butter-milk in the bowl of a food processor and pulse for 90 seconds. In a large bowl, combine the flour, salt, baking powder, and cayenne. Fold the corn mixture and the crabmeat into the dry ingredients and mix until well incorporated.

2 In a separate bowl, beat the egg whites until stiff peaks form. Fold the beaten egg whites into the crab and corn mixture.

3 Preheat the oven to 200°F.

4 Preheat a large skillet over medium-high heat and add the oil. When the oil is hot, reduce the heat to medium. Spoon 2 table-spoons of batter for each fritter into the pan. Cook for 3 to 4 minutes on each side, until the fritters are golden brown. Remove them from the pan, place them on a baking sheet, and keep them warm in the oven. Serve them on top of Cucumber-Watercress Salad (recipe follows).

Cucumber-Watercress Salad

FOR THE SALAD:

1 small red onion, peeled and very thinly sliced

1 cucumber, peeled and very thinly sliced

1 bunch watercress, stems trimmed

2 oranges, cut into sections (page 27)

FOR THE DRESSING:

3 tablespoons Greek yogurt

1 tablespoon fresh lemon juice

1 tablespoon fresh orange juice

1 tablespoon tarragon vinegar

1 teaspoon honey

2 shallots, minced

2 tablespoons chopped fresh mint

Salt and freshly ground black pepper

1 To make the salad, combine the onion, cucumber, watercress, and orange segments in a large bowl.

2 To make the dressing, whisk together the yogurt, lemon juice, orange juice, vinegar, honey, shallots, and mint in a small bowl. Season with salt and pepper to taste. Toss with the salad and serve.

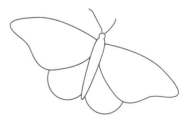

Roasted Capon and Endive

A capon (a young rooster) is the juiciest bird, very flavorful and tender. It works perfectly with this recipe, but if you can't find capon at your local butcher shop, you can use chicken. A lot of great organic farms raise capons, which are delicious with the organic wine paired with this dish. Serve this dish with plenty of crusty bread to sop up the delicious juices.

1 tablespoon fresh thyme leaves

1 tablespoon chopped fresh chives

1 tablespoon chopped fresh flat-leaf parsley

1 tablespoon chopped fresh tarragon

1 cup (2 sticks) butter, at room temperature

1 orange (zest, juice, and what's left of the flesh)

1 lemon (zest, juice, and what's left of the flesh)

5 garlic cloves, minced

3 teaspoons salt, plus more to season capon

1 teaspoon paprika

¼ cup ground raw almonds

1 Combine the thyme, chives, parsley, and tarragon; set aside 2 tablespoons of this mixture for the stuffing. Combine the remaining herb mixture with the butter, orange and lemon zests, minced garlic, 2 teaspoons of the salt, the paprika, and ground almonds in the bowl of a food processor and puree until smooth. Refrigerate for 10 minutes to allow the butter to firm up.

2 Prepare a basting marinade by whisking together the lemon and orange juices, wine, brown sugar, and 3 of the crushed garlic cloves in a small bowl. Set aside.

3 Prepare the stuffing by combining the chopped flesh of the orange and lemon, the remaining 3 crushed garlic cloves, the remaining 1 teaspoon salt, the pepper, and the 2 tablespoons of reserved herbs in a small bowl. Mix well.

4 Preheat the oven to 400°F.

Crab-Corn Fritters with Cucumber-Watercress Salad, PAGE 146

Endive, Roasted Red Pepper, and Black Olive Salad, PAGE 158

Watermelon Sorbet with Fresh Basil, PAGE 150

Vidalia Onion, Cèpe, and Arugula Tarts, PAGE 134

L'Espalier's Fried Chicken and Honey Biscuits, PAGE 137

Grilled Rib-Eye Steaks with Frank's Potato Gratin, PAGE 115

Vegetable Gratin with Tomato-Saffron Coulis, PAGE 111

Bittersweet Chocolate Terrine with Warm Pumpkin Sauce
and Shaved Black Truffle, PAGE 200

1 cup Pinot Noir

1 tablespoon brown sugar

6 garlic cloves, crushed

½ teaspoon freshly ground black pepper, plus more to season capon

1 whole capon (about 7 pounds)

6 shallots

3 heads endive, cut in half lengthwise

3 garlic cloves, whole

5 Spread the butter mixture liberally under the skin of the entire breast and lower thigh of the capon. Insert the stuffing into the capon cavity. Truss the legs together with butcher twine (below).

6 Place the capon, breast side up, in a medium-size roasting pan (one in which the capon fits snugly). Arrange the shallots, endive halves, and the whole garlic cloves around the sides of the capon.

7 Pour the basting marinade over the capon, dust the bird with salt, and roast for 2 hours, turning every 24 minutes (on its side, on its breast, on its other side, then breast side up again). Baste the bird each time you turn it, adding additional liquid (water or wine) to maintain the original liquid level. For the final 24 minutes of cooking (breast side up), reduce the oven temperature to 350°F. Remove the capon from the oven and transfer it to a serving platter.

8 Strain the pan juices into a sauceboat, skim off the fat, and season with salt and pepper to taste. Carve the capon and serve with the endive and shallots and drizzled with the cooking juices.

TRUSSING

The point of trussing chicken and other poultry is not to create more work, but to help maintain moisture and keep the meat juicy. Simply hold the legs together and tie firmly with a piece of butcher's twine at the legs' midpoint.

Watermelon Sorbet with Fresh Basil

There's nothing more refreshing than watermelon in summer, and to have the essence of watermelon chilled into a sorbet is tremendous. For best results, use very sweet watermelon. Basil works so well with watermelon—it has an aromatic richness that complements the sweet, fresh watermelon flavor.

4 cups ½-inch watermelon cubes
   (2 pounds watermelon flesh)

½ cup plus 1 tablespoon sugar

½ teaspoon rose water (optional)

12 basil leaves, cut into
   chiffonade (page 101)

1 Place the watermelon cubes on a baking sheet lined with several layers of paper towels. Cover and refrigerate for at least 6 hours to drain.

2 Puree the drained watermelon in a blender with the sugar and rose water, if using. Freeze the sorbet in an ice cream maker according to the manufacturer's instructions. Garnish with the basil before serving.

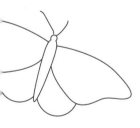

ITALY

I couldn't write a book about food and wine without including Italy. It's a country that has had a tremendous impact on food all over the world, and it has one of the longest wine-growing histories of any country. Besides that, I am personally drawn to Italian food and wine. I like it so much that a lot of people think I'm part Italian, but I'm actually all Scottish. The combinations and compositions of vegetables, fruits, starches, and meats in Italian cuisine are so wholesome and heartwarming, and Italian wine is easy to drink with any meal. My favorite dinner on a Sunday night is without question an Italian dinner, with a nice (and usually nicely affordable) bottle of Italian wine.

MENU

& pairings

↓

 +

PAIRINGS

1

Endive, Roasted
Red Pepper, and
Black Olive Salad

2004 Mastroberardino,
"Nova Serra," Greco di Tufo,
Campania

2

Giant Caponata Ravioli

2004 Schiavenza,
Barbera d'Alba,
Piedmont

3

Osso Buco with
Fava Beans

2001 Musso,
"Pora," Barbaresco,
Piedmont

4

Amarone-Poached Figs
with Mascarpone Cream

2002 Villa Erbice,
Recioto di Soave,
Veneto

WINE NOTES

↓

1ST PAIRING **ENDIVE, ROASTED RED PEPPER, AND BLACK OLIVE SALAD**
SERVED WITH → 2004 MASTROBERARDINO, "NOVA SERRA," GRECO DI TUFO, CAMPANIA

Greco di Tufo is a very old grape variety, originally from Greece. It makes an aromatic and snappy white wine that plays well against the mix of flavors and textures in this salad. A Pinot Grigio would also do the trick.

2ND PAIRING **GIANT CAPONATA RAVIOLI**
SERVED WITH → 2004 SCHIAVENZA, BARBERA D'ALBA, PIEDMONT

This wine has a plummy, dried-fruit flavor that's soft enough to let the flavors of the caponata and the texture of the pasta be the stars. Chianti would be another good choice to go with this ravioli.

3RD PAIRING **OSSO BUCO WITH FAVA BEANS**
SERVED WITH → 2001 MUSSO, "PORA," BARBARESCO, PIEDMONT

Nebbiolo is the grape variety in this wine, as well as in Barolo, which is considered the king of Italian reds. This is a more refined interpretation of Nebbiolo; you could certainly also pair a Barolo with this dish if you wanted to.

4TH PAIRING **AMARONE-POACHED FIGS WITH MASCARPONE CREAM**
SERVED WITH → 2002 VILLA ERBICE, RECIOTO DI SOAVE, VENETO

We tried this dessert wine from Soave recently and loved it, so we introduced it to guests of L'Espalier. Soave is usually a light, dry white wine, but in this case the fruit hung around on the vine for a while and gathered a nice concentration of sweetness. Cream sherry and tawny port are also delicious with this dessert.

Endive, Roasted Red Pepper, and Black Olive Salad

This salad features a typical Italian combination of bitter greens, sweet vegetables (and raisins), and salty olives. Creamy mozzarella and crunchy multigrain crostini round out the dish, helping the flavors come together to make a great starter salad.

¼ cup golden raisins

1 navel orange, cut into sections (page 27), juice reserved

¼ cup balsamic vinegar

5 tablespoons extra virgin olive oil

1 teaspoon mustard

1 teaspoon minced garlic

1 teaspoon chopped fresh basil

Salt and freshly ground black pepper

3 heads endive

3 red bell peppers, roasted (page 161) and quartered

½ cup pitted and chopped kalamata olives

½ red onion, thinly sliced

One 6-ounce ball buffalo mozzarella, sliced lengthwise into 5 pieces, then cut into strips

6 large multigrain crostini (at right)

1 Combine the raisins, reserved orange juice, and balsamic vinegar in a small bowl. Let the raisins soak for 30 minutes. Drain the raisins and set aside; reserve the marinating liquid.

2 Whisk the olive oil, mustard, garlic, basil, marinating liquid, salt, and pepper together in a large bowl.

3 Cut the endive heads in half and then slice them thinly into sticks. Add the sliced endive, roasted peppers, olives, onion, orange segments, and soaked raisins to the bowl and toss.

4 Add the mozzarella strips to the bowl. Toss again. Divide the salad among 6 bowls and top with the crostini.

MULTIGRAIN CROSTINI
You can find prepared multigrain crostini at many gourmet and grocery stores, but if you want to prepare your own, rub a crushed garlic clove on six ¾-inch-thick slices of multigrain baguette. Brush the baguette slices on both sides with olive oil, dust with salt and pepper, place on a baking sheet, and bake in a 375°F oven for 13 minutes, or until golden brown but still chewy.

Giant Caponata Ravioli

You can't go wrong if you have ravioli on your menu. I don't know anyone who doesn't like it (and I crave it). It's fun to make one giant round ravioli for each guest, but you could also make smaller ravioli or play around with shapes. Have some fun! Making your own pasta dough isn't hard, but to save time you could purchase premade pasta sheets. In Italy the pasta, not the sauce, is the focal point of the dish, and that's how we present these ravioli, with just a little olive oil and grated cheese.

1 medium-size eggplant

1½ teaspoons salt

½ teaspoon dried basil

½ cup olive oil

1 large white onion, thinly sliced

1 celery stalk, sliced

1 cup drained and chopped canned Italian plum tomatoes

2 tablespoons capers, rinsed and drained

2 red bell peppers, roasted (page 161) and chopped

3 garlic cloves, minced

14 black olives, pitted and chopped

¼ cup pine nuts, toasted

1 Peel the eggplant and cut it into 1-inch cubes. Toss with 1 teaspoon of the salt and the dried basil and let stand in a colander for 30 minutes to 1 hour to release the excess liquid. Heat a medium-size frying pan over medium-high heat. When it's hot, add enough olive oil to coat the pan. When the oil is hot, add the eggplant and reduce the heat to medium. Brown the eggplant on all sides, about 5 minutes total. Remove it from the pan with a slotted spoon and set aside.

2 Add the remaining olive oil to the pan. When the oil is hot, add the onion and cook until golden brown, about 4 minutes, stirring constantly. Add the celery and cook for 3 minutes. Add the tomatoes, capers, roasted peppers, garlic, olives, and pine nuts. Stir to distribute evenly in the pan. Cover and reduce the heat to low. Let simmer for 10 minutes, checking often to make sure nothing burns. (If it looks like it's about to burn, add a bit of water to the pan.)

(continued)

¼ cup red wine vinegar

¼ cup sugar

½ teaspoon freshly ground black pepper

¼ teaspoon cayenne pepper

2 tablespoons chopped fresh flat-leaf parsley

1 tablespoon store-bought pesto

Pasta Dough (recipe follows)

1 large egg white, lightly beaten with 1 teaspoon water

Extra virgin olive oil

6 tablespoons freshly grated Parmesan cheese

3 Uncover the pan and add the vinegar, sugar, the remaining ½ teaspoon salt, the black pepper, cayenne, and parsley. Stir, cover, and cook for 5 minutes, again watching carefully to make sure nothing burns. Transfer the browned eggplant to the bowl of a food processor, add the pesto, and pulse for 1 minute, until blended but still coarse. Check for seasoning and adjust if needed. Allow to cool completely.

4 To make the ravioli, if you're using a pasta machine, roll out the pasta dough on the thinnest setting. If using a rolling pin, dust the countertop with flour, place half the dough on the counter, and continually roll and flip it until it is as thin as possible.

5 To form the ravioli, cut out 4-inch rounds (or any shape you like) with a cookie cutter. Work with 2 rounds at a time. Brush them both on one side with the beaten egg white. Place a heaping tablespoon of the eggplant mixture in the center of the egg-washed side of one pasta round and press the other round on top, egg-washed side down. Seal all the edges with your fingers. Set aside on a floured baking sheet while you make the rest of the ravioli. You can make the ravioli up to this point and refrigerate them for 1 day or freeze them for up to 1 month.

6 When all your ravioli are made, fill a medium-size pot about halfway with salted water and bring to a boil. When the water is boiling, add the ravioli. They are done when they float to the top of the water, about 3 minutes.

7 Serve them with a drizzle of your best extra virgin olive oil and a sprinkling of the Parmesan cheese.

Pasta Dough

1 cup durum semolina flour

1 cup all-purpose flour

1 teaspoon salt

4 large egg yolks

1 large egg

¼ teaspoon olive oil

2 teaspoons milk

1 Combine the flours and salt in the bowl of an electric mixer. Beat the yolks, egg, olive oil, and milk into the dry ingredients until combined.

2 Knead on a lightly floured surface for 3 to 4 minutes. Wrap tightly in plastic wrap and let rest for 1 hour or up to overnight in the refrigerator before using.

ROASTED RED PEPPERS

It's easy to make your own roasted red peppers. Preheat the oven to 450°F. Slice the peppers in half and core them. Toss them with olive oil and salt and pepper and roast them on a baking sheet for 30 to 35 minutes. Remove the peppers from the oven and place them in a bowl, covered with plastic wrap, until they are cool enough to touch. Remove the skin as much as you can—it should come off pretty easily.

Osso Buco with Fava Beans

Anyone who says veal is bland hasn't tried this classic Italian preparation. These luscious shanks melt in your mouth, and they go beautifully with lemon- and garlic-scented fava beans and a bold red wine.

6 veal shanks

2 garlic cloves, crushed

Zest and juice of 1 orange

1 teaspoon dried oregano

1 teaspoon dried thyme

¼ cup vegetable oil

3 tablespoons all-purpose flour

Salt and freshly ground black pepper

1 large white onion, diced

3 carrots, peeled and diced

3 celery stalks, diced

1 leek, cut in half, washed (page 195), and diced

8 garlic cloves, minced

4 ounces fresh porcini mushrooms, or ¾ ounce dried porcini, reconstituted (page 91), thinly sliced

1 cup Madeira

2 cups white wine

1 Rub the veal shanks with the crushed garlic and orange zest. Sprinkle the shanks with the oregano and thyme and let stand for 30 minutes to 1 hour.

2 Preheat the oven to 325°F.

3 Heat a large, deep ovenproof skillet or braising pan over medium-high heat. When the pan is hot, add the oil. Place the flour in a broad, shallow plate or pan. When the oil is hot, season the shanks with salt and pepper, dust them with the flour, and add them to the pan. Cook until golden brown, about 3 to 4 minutes, then turn.

4 After you've turned the shanks, add the onion to the pan around the shanks and cook for 3 minutes, stirring with a wooden spoon. Add the carrots, celery, and leek, and cook for 3 minutes, stirring. Add the minced garlic and cook for 30 seconds. Add the mushrooms, stir, and cook for 3 minutes. Add the Madeira and cook for 1 minute. Add the white wine and cook for 3 minutes.

2 quarts chicken broth

1 Parmesan rind (about 2 inches by 1 inch)

2 tablespoons tomato paste

2 cups seeded and chopped plum tomatoes

3 bay leaves

2 whole cloves

1 teaspoon saffron

5 Add the broth, Parmesan rind, tomato paste, and tomatoes and bring to a slight simmer. Skim off any debris that forms on top, using a ladle. Add the bay leaves and cloves, cover, and bake in the oven for 1½ hours, or until the meat is very tender. Remove from the oven, uncover, add the saffron, and check the seasoning, adjusting if necessary. Serve with Fava Beans (recipe follows).

Fava Beans

2 cups fresh or frozen fava beans

2 tablespoons butter

1 tablespoon olive oil

1 garlic clove, minced

1 tablespoon fresh lemon juice

Salt and freshly ground black pepper

1 Blanch the fava beans in boiling water for 1 minute, then shock them in cold water to stop the cooking. Peel the fava beans.

2 Heat a medium-size saucepan over medium heat. Add the butter and olive oil to the pan. When the butter is bubbling, add the garlic and cook for 2 minutes.

3 Add the fava beans, lemon juice, salt, and pepper to the pan and toss. When bubbling, after about 4 minutes, remove the beans from the pan and serve.

Amarone-Poached Figs
with Mascarpone Cream

I love amarone, a robust Italian red wine made from semi-dried grapes, and I love figs. Amarone has a raisiny, port-like flavor that's delicious with figs and cheese. This simple dessert brings it all together.

---

2 cups amarone

1 cup sugar

Zest of 1 orange

1 tablespoon cardamom pods

3 segments of a star anise pod

2 cups fresh black Mission figs

1 Combine the amarone, sugar, orange zest, cardamom, and star anise in a medium-size saucepan and cook over medium heat until the sugar dissolves, about 4 minutes.

2 Cut the stems off the figs. Use a paring knife to cut a ¾-inch strip of skin away from the center of the fig, leaving only the top and bottom of the fig with skin.

3 Add the figs to the poaching liquid and cook over medium heat until the liquid has a syrupy consistency, about 10 minutes. Serve in small bowls with dollops of Mascarpone Cream (recipe follows).

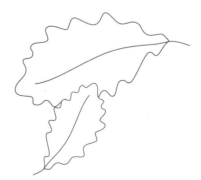

Mascarpone Cream

½ cup plus 2 tablespoons light
  cream

¼ cup sugar

2 large egg yolks

5 ounces mascarpone cheese

1 Heat the cream in a small saucepan o
medium heat for about 3 minutes, or
just hot. In a separate bowl, whisk the
and egg yolks together. When the crea
hot, remove it from the heat and pour
gradually into the egg mixture, stirring
being careful not to cook the eggs. Wh
the cream is added, pour the mixture b
into the saucepan and cook over mediu
heat, stirring with a rubber spatula, unt
the mixture is thick enough to coat the
of a spoon. An instant-read thermomete
dipped into it should read 160°F.

2 Remove from the heat and pour into a
mixing bowl. Let cool until it's warm bu
not hot to the touch. Place the mascarpo
in a separate bowl and pour the egg mixtu
over it. Whisk until well combined. Let c
completely in the refrigerator; serve chille

HALLOW-WINE: GHOSTLY GLASSES AND DEVILISH DELIGHTS

The dishes on this menu and the wines paired with them are delicious, of course, but they are also playful enough for an occasion like Halloween, which certainly doesn't call for being too serious. Eating food and drinking wine are great pleasures—so don't be afraid to have fun when planning a menu and selecting wines! I love planning dinners for wacky holidays, and

Halloween is one of my favorites. I host a Halloween party every year and cook for at least 30 kids—the event has become legendary in my neighborhood. Halloween is near harvest time, so it's a great food time of year. Pomegranates are just coming into season, pecans and chestnuts are fresh, and there are lots of apples around.

MENU

& pairings

↓

+

PAIRINGS

**Frankenstein McClelland's
Blood-Red Pomegranate
and Goat Cheese Salad**

1

**2000 Barmès Buecher,
"Herrenweg de Turckheim,"
Riesling, Alsace, France**

**Witches' Bubbling Broth of
Braised Werewolf Fish with
Coconut-Lemongrass Rice**

2

**2003 Château d'Aqueria,
Rosé, Tavel, Rhône,
France**

**Grilled Pork Tenderloin with
Gooey Polenta and Haunted
Forest Mushrooms**

3

**2003 Thunder Mountain,
Bates Ranch, Meritage,
Santa Cruz, California**

**Dark Chocolate Ice Cream
with Candied Chestnuts**

4

**2004 Rosa Regale,
Brachetto d'Acqui,
Piedmont, Italy**

WINE ⬚ NOTES

↓

1ST PAIRING **FRANKENSTEIN MCCLELLAND'S BLOOD-RED POMEGRANATE AND GOAT CHEESE SALAD**
SERVED WITH → **2000 BARMÈS BUECHER, "HERRENWEG DE TURCKHEIM," RIESLING, ALSACE, FRANCE**

First of all, the name of this wine (Herrenweg de Turckheim) sounds like it could be an angry villager character in a scary monster story—and that's certainly a good reason to choose a wine for a Halloween dinner. Beyond that, we chose this because Riesling is a perfumey, aromatic grape variety with great flavor and nice acidity that works well with the richness of goat cheese and the tartness of pomegranate seeds. German Rieslings tend to run to the sweet side, but Rieslings from Alsace tend to be very dry—so if you want dry Riesling, get it from Alsace. You could also try a Riesling or a Pinot Grigio from the Pacific Northwest. Barmès Buecher is a wonderful small wine producer, but there are plenty of other delicious Rieslings from the region.

2ND PAIRING **WITCHES' BUBBLING BROTH OF BRAISED WEREWOLF FISH WITH COCONUT-LEMONGRASS RICE**
SERVED WITH → **2003 CHÂTEAU D'AQUERIA, ROSÉ, TAVEL, RHÔNE, FRANCE**

We wanted to serve rosé on this menu because for so many people it's a scary wine! We've seen guests recoil in horror when they see pink, because they expect it to be so sticky sweet. In fact, most rosés are dry, and for wine drinkers who enjoy both red and white, they offer the best of both worlds: the crisp, refreshing qualities of a white and the earthiness and spiciness of a red. Combined, those qualities work really well with food. A dry rosé is a good choice with this dish because of the earthy, slightly spicy flavor of the curry, tamarind, and mushrooms.

3RD PAIRING **GRILLED PORK TENDERLOIN WITH GOOEY POLENTA AND HAUNTED FOREST MUSHROOMS**
SERVED WITH → **2003 THUNDER MOUNTAIN, BATES RANCH, MERITAGE, SANTA CRUZ, CALIFORNIA**

Have you ever chosen a bottle of wine because of the label? So have we. This wine has a somewhat scary label that's perfect for Halloween. Plus, the wine is really good. It's a blend of Bordeaux grape varieties grown in Santa Cruz, which has a cooler growing climate than Napa and Sonoma. That means the fruit isn't quite as ripe, and the result is a wine that is lighter than typical California cabernets, but with lots of flavor and a soft, round, velvety finish. It works well with the sweet earthiness of the mushrooms. A Barbera from Italy or a Grenache would be a good alternative.

This is a beautiful sparkling red wine that tastes great with chocolate (especially when the chocolate isn't too sweet, as in the case of this dark chocolate ice cream). Plus, its dark red, bubbling appearance is definitely right for Halloween. Another brand of Brachetto would work, as would a port or Banyuls.

HOW TO SEED A POMEGRANATE

I know people who've been cooking for decades who still struggle with seeding pomegranates, but it can be easy. Cut the pomegranate in half through the widest part of the fruit, then turn the flesh side against your open hand so the seeds can fall easily through your fingers. Holding the pomegranate over a bowl, use the back of a large metal serving spoon to pound the round part of the pomegranate, until all the seeds have fallen out and into the bowl. It should take a minute or two to get all the seeds out.

Frankenstein McClelland's
Blood-Red Pomegranate
and Goat Cheese Salad

The sweet, deep acidity of the pomegranate seeds cuts through the richness of the creamy goat cheese and plays off the nuttiness of the pecans. The anise flavor of the fennel rounds out this salad.

8 ounces (about 10 cups) baby
    spinach

Seeds of 2 pomegranates
    (about 2 cups; facing page)

2 apples (preferably Cortland or
    Lady), peeled, cored, and diced

1 small red onion, thinly shaved

1 small fennel bulb, thinly
    shaved

1 cup pecan halves, toasted
    (below)

Pomegranate Vinaigrette
    (page 172)

12 ounces fresh goat cheese

In a large bowl, toss the spinach with the pomegranate seeds, apples, onion, fennel, pecans, and vinaigrette. Crumble the goat cheese on top and gently toss again. Serve immediately.

TOASTING NUTS

Toasting nuts brings out their best flavor. To toast them lightly, spread them evenly on a baking sheet and bake for 5 minutes in a 400°F oven. For more intense toasted flavor, bake for 8 to 10 minutes.

Pomegranate Vinaigrette

3 tablespoons pomegranate juice

2 tablespoons apple cider

1 teaspoon Dijon mustard

1 garlic clove, minced

1 teaspoon fresh lemon juice

1 teaspoon balsamic vinegar

1 teaspoon fresh thyme leaves

1 teaspoon freshly ground black pepper

1 teaspoon salt

½ teaspoon light soy sauce

¼ cup plus 2 tablespoons olive oil

¼ cup canola oil

In a small bowl, mix together the pomegranate juice, cider, mustard, garlic, lemon juice, vinegar, thyme, pepper, salt, and soy sauce. In a separate bowl, blend together the olive and canola oils. Pour the blended oil into the juice mixture in a slow stream, whisking constantly. Adjust the seasoning to taste if necessary.

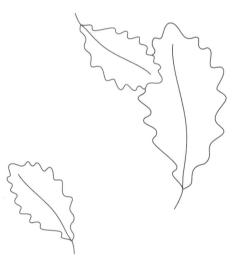

Witches' Bubbling Broth of Braised Werewolf Fish with Coconut-Lemongrass Rice

When we served this dish at a Hallow-Wine Monday, one of our guests told us she'd never heard of werewolf fish. Just to be clear, it's wolf fish—we just had a little fun with the names of dishes on this menu. Wolf fish is also known as ocean catfish. When choosing wine for your bubbling broth, save the really good wine to drink. While it's true that you should try to cook only with wine you'd actually drink, an inexpensive wine (think "two-buck Chuck" Sauvignon Blanc, which I would actually drink) is just fine for cooking here. In the fall I love cooking with local apple cider—if you can, look for cider at a farm stand near you.

1 teaspoon yellow curry paste

1 teaspoon tamarind paste

Zest of 1 lemon

1¼ pounds wolf fish (ocean catfish) fillets, cut into 6 pieces

Salt and freshly ground black pepper

2 tablespoons vegetable oil

1 medium-size yellow onion, diced

3 garlic cloves, minced

6 shiitake mushrooms, thinly sliced

¼ cup sherry

½ cup white wine

1 tablespoon fresh lemon juice

⅓ cup apple cider

½ cup heavy cream

1   Combine the curry paste, tamarind paste, and lemon zest in a small bowl. Smear the mixture evenly over the fish fillets and let them rest in the refrigerator, covered with plastic wrap, for 2 to 3 hours.

2   Preheat the oven to 400°F.

3   Preheat a large ovenproof sauté pan over medium-high heat for about 2 minutes. Remove the fish from the refrigerator and season the fillets with salt and pepper. Add the oil to the pan and heat for about 30 seconds (don't let it burn). Add the fillets to the pan and cook for 2 to 3 minutes on each side, until golden brown.

4   Remove the fillets from the pan and set aside. Add the onion to the pan and cook for 2 to 3 minutes, stirring often with a wooden spoon. Add the garlic and mushrooms and cook for 1 minute, stirring occasionally. Add the sherry and cook for 2 minutes. Add the white wine and cook for another 2 minutes. Return the fillets to the

(continued)

pan. Add the lemon juice, cider, and heavy cream and bring to a simmer. Transfer the pan to the oven. Depending upon the thickness of the fillets, bake for 8 to 12 minutes (about 8 minutes for a ½-inch fillet; 12 minutes for a ¾-inch fillet).

5 Remove the pan from the oven, lift the fillets from the pan with a spatula, and place them on a platter. Place the pan back on the stove over medium heat and cook for 1 to 2 minutes, until the sauce thickens slightly but is still fluid enough to pour easily. Spoon the sauce from the pan over the fillets. Serve with Coconut-Lemongrass Rice (recipe follows).

Coconut-Lemongrass Rice

Soaking the rice before cooking helps to pull some of the starch out of the rice, resulting in grains that are more tender. This is a simple and flavorful side dish that would work well with many chicken dishes and main courses with Asian-inspired flavors.

1½ cups jasmine rice

1 tablespoon butter

1 garlic clove, crushed

1 tablespoon grated fresh ginger

½ stalk lemongrass, chopped into 2 pieces and crushed with the back of a chef's knife

2 cups water

One 16-ounce can coconut milk

2 teaspoons salt

Soak the rice for 20 minutes in salted water to cover, then drain. Melt the butter in a large saucepan over medium heat. Add the garlic, ginger, lemongrass, and rice and toast the rice for 2 minutes, stirring with a wooden spoon. Add the water, coconut milk, and salt. Cover and reduce the heat to low. Cook for 20 minutes, or until all the liquid is absorbed.

Grilled Pork Tenderloin
with Gooey Polenta and
Haunted Forest Mushrooms

When I was growing up, fall was the time when we would slaughter pigs on our farm—so I always associate pork with autumn. Grilling the pork gives it a sweet smokiness that complements the mushrooms and the polenta that round out this menu.

2 garlic cloves, chopped

½ teaspoon paprika

¼ teaspoon ground cloves

½ teaspoon dried thyme

1 tablespoon maple syrup

1 tablespoon balsamic vinegar

1 teaspoon Worcestershire sauce

½ teaspoon freshly ground black pepper

2 pork tenderloins (about 1 pound each)

1 In a medium-size bowl, mix together the garlic, paprika, cloves, thyme, maple syrup, vinegar, Worcestershire sauce, and black pepper. Rub the mixture all over the tenderloins and marinate the pork, covered, in the refrigerator for 3 hours or overnight. Remove the pork from the refrigerator 1 hour before cooking.

2 Prepare a medium-hot fire in a charcoal grill. Or, preheat a gas grill on high for 10 minutes before grilling, then reduce the heat to medium-high. Grill the pork for 12 to 15 minutes, turning the pork every 3 minutes. Remove the pork from the grill and let sit for 5 minutes, covered with aluminum foil to keep the heat in. Slice the pork and serve it over Gooey Polenta, topped with Haunted Forest Mushrooms (page 176).

Gooey Polenta

3 tablespoons butter

1 shallot, minced

2 garlic cloves, minced

1 quart chicken broth

1 cup cornmeal

¼ cup freshly grated Parmesan cheese

Salt and freshly ground black pepper

1 Melt the butter in a large saucepan over medium-high heat. Sauté the shallot and garlic in the butter for about 2 minutes. Add the broth and bring to a boil. Add the cornmeal and stir continually for 3 to 4 minutes. When it just starts bubbling, reduce the heat to low and stir every 4 to 5 minutes for about 30 minutes, until the polenta starts to pull away from the sides of the pan.

2 Remove the pan from the heat and stir in the cheese, salt, and pepper.

Haunted Forest Mushrooms

1 tablespoon butter

1 tablespoon olive oil

½ small yellow onion, chopped

3 garlic cloves, chopped

½ pound mushrooms (a mix of cremini, lobster, porcini, chanterelle, portobello, etc.), sliced

¼ cup Madeira

1 cup peeled (page 123), seeded, and chopped tomatoes

1 teaspoon dried tarragon

Salt and freshly ground black pepper

1 Heat a large sauté pan over medium-high heat. Add the butter and oil to the pan and heat until sizzling, about 1 minute. Add the onion and cook until translucent, about 3 minutes. Add the garlic and cook, stirring, for about 30 seconds.

2 Add the mushrooms and cook until they start to sweat, 3 to 4 minutes.

3 Add the Madeira and cook until absorbed, about 1½ minutes. Add the tomatoes and tarragon, reduce the heat to low, and cover.

4 Cook for 5 to 7 minutes, until the mushrooms are tender and the mixture is bubbling. Season with salt and pepper to taste before serving.

Dark Chocolate Ice Cream
with Candied Chestnuts

Grownups like chocolate and candy on Halloween, too, so this menu includes a deep, dark chocolate ice cream that is accented with the sweetness of candied chestnuts. There aren't many ingredients in the ice cream, so the chocolate you use really makes a difference. I like to use Valrhona or another high-quality chocolate.

2 cups milk

⅓ cup sugar

1 cup coarsely chopped bittersweet chocolate

3 tablespoons unsweetened cocoa powder

1 vanilla bean, split lengthwise and scraped

5 large egg yolks

1 Prepare an ice bath (page 21).

2 Combine the milk, sugar, chocolate, cocoa powder, and vanilla bean pod and scrapings in a medium-size saucepan. Bring to a simmer over medium-high heat.

3 Reduce the heat to low. Place the egg yolks in a medium-size bowl and whisk about ½ cup of the hot liquid into the yolks to temper them. When well incorporated, pour the yolk mixture back into the saucepan and stir the mixture constantly with a wooden spoon until it's thick enough to coat a spoon, about 5 minutes (180°F on an instant-read thermometer). Strain the mixture through a fine-mesh sieve into a medium-size bowl. Place the bowl into the ice bath and stir the mixture until it has cooled.

4 Freeze the mixture in an ice cream maker according to the manufacturer's instructions. Serve topped with Candied Chestnuts (page 178).

Candied Chestnuts

1 cup water

½ cup sugar

1 cup roasted chestnuts (below)

2 tablespoons candied ginger

½ teaspoon ground cinnamon

¼ teaspoon salt

1 Preheat the oven to 350°F. Grease a baking sheet.

2 Bring the water and sugar to a boil in a medium-size saucepan. Add the chestnuts, ginger, cinnamon, and salt. Cook over medium-high heat until the syrup is thick enough to coat the nuts, 6 to 7 minutes, stirring often to make sure the nuts are well coated. Transfer the nuts to the baking sheet and bake for about 10 minutes, until the nuts are a golden caramel brown.

3 Remove from the oven and let cool on a wire rack.

ROASTING CHESTNUTS

When buying fresh chestnuts, look for nuts that are firm and unblemished. Preheat the oven to 350°F. Use a sharp knife to make an X on each chestnut, slicing through the shell but not into the meat. (Do not skip this step, or the chestnuts will explode in the oven!) Arrange them in a single layer on a baking sheet and roast for 25 to 35 minutes (the larger the chestnuts, the longer the roasting time). Let cool, then peel and rub off all the skins. You can roast the chestnuts a couple of days in advance and store them at room temperature in an airtight container.

SPAIN

The hills of Spain are fragrant with the smells of saffron, olive oil, and vineyards ripening, and the food of Spain features lively spices and rich flavors. These flavors make your palate sing and become so entwined with the taste of the wine that it's a pleasure to eat and have a gulp of wine almost at the same moment. Spain is one of the largest wine-producing countries in the world. It produces exquisite, affordable wines in many different regions, so there's a lot of accessible wine to explore. The best known is Rioja, where Tempranillo and Garnacha are the main grape varieties used, but there are dozens of others—and Spain is also renowned for its sherry.

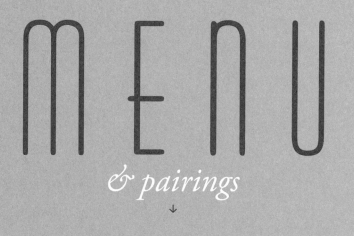

AUTUMN → Spain

MENU

& pairings

↓

 +

PAIRINGS

White Asparagus and Blood Orange Salad	**1**	**Covides, "Gran Gesta," Brut Rosé, Cava, Penedés, Catalonia**
Saffron-Braised Squid with Ragoût of White Beans, Chorizo, and Rosemary	**2**	**2005 Nora, Albariño, Rías Baixas, Galicia**
Rioja-Roasted Lamb with Chickpeas, Black Olives, and Escarole	**3**	**2005 Atteca, "Old Vines," Garnacha, Calatayud, Aragón**
Rice Pudding with Raisins and Pine Nuts	**4**	**Emilio Lustau, "East India Solera," Cream Sherry, Andalucía**

WINE 🍷 NOTES

↓

1ST PAIRING **WHITE ASPARAGUS AND BLOOD ORANGE SALAD**
SERVED WITH → COVIDES, "GRAN GESTA," BRUT ROSÉ, CAVA, PENEDÉS, CATALONIA

Cava is the sparkling wine of Spain, and it's fantastic and much less expensive than Champagne. High-quality rosé cava is harder to find than excellent standard cava, but this is a good one. If you can't find it or another rosé cava, try one of those tasty regular cavas.

2ND PAIRING **SAFFRON-BRAISED SQUID WITH RAGOÛT OF WHITE BEANS, CHORIZO, AND ROSEMARY**
SERVED WITH → 2005 NORA, ALBARIÑO, RÍAS BAIXAS, GALICIA

Albariño and seafood is a classic pairing. The white wine is aromatic and a little salty and practically cries out for seafood. An unoaked Sauvignon Blanc from a cool climate such as the Loire or New Zealand would also complement this dish.

3RD PAIRING **RIOJA-ROASTED LAMB WITH CHICKPEAS, BLACK OLIVES, AND ESCAROLE**
SERVED WITH → 2005 ATTECA, "OLD VINES," GARNACHA, CALATAYUD, ARAGÓN

This Garnacha (AKA Grenache) is made from grapes grown on vines that are more than a century old, and the flavor is thick, deep, and concentrated—yet it still has good balance and isn't too heavy. The lamb would also be delicious with a Grenache from California or Australia, or a Syrah.

4TH PAIRING **RICE PUDDING WITH RAISINS AND PINE NUTS**
SERVED WITH → EMILIO LUSTAU, "EAST INDIA SOLERA," CREAM SHERRY, ANDALUCÍA

Spain is famous for its sherry. This one has a beautifully sweet nuttiness. When pairing wine with dessert, you generally want the wine to be sweeter than the food, so another dessert wine like Muscat also would work well here.

White Asparagus and Blood Orange Salad

The sweetness of the asparagus and the saltiness of the anchovies along with the sweet acidity of the citrus create a wonderful juxtaposition of flavors in your mouth. White asparagus is a traditional item on tapas menus in Spain, and the other ingredients in this salad are often found in Spanish cuisine.

1 pound white asparagus, trimmed (page 184)

2 cups milk

1 vanilla bean, split lengthwise and scraped

2 bay leaves

1 teaspoon fresh oregano

1 teaspoon salt

4 black peppercorns

1 tablespoon sugar

½ cup Marcona almonds

2 heads frisée

Blood Orange Vinaigrette (page 184)

3 blood oranges, cut into sections (page 27)

18 marinated white anchovies

1 Preheat the oven to 350°F.

2 Place the asparagus, milk, vanilla bean pod and scrapings, bay leaves, oregano, salt, peppercorns, and sugar in a medium-size ovenproof pot big enough to lay the asparagus down flat and submerge it in the milk.

3 Bring the milk mixture to a simmer over medium-low heat, then cover the pot with aluminum foil. Bake in the oven until tender, about 25 minutes. Remove the asparagus from the oven, remove the foil, and allow the asparagus to cool in its liquid in the refrigerator.

4 Spread the almonds on a baking sheet and toast in the oven for about 8 minutes, or until golden brown. Remove from the oven and set aside to cool.

5 Lightly season the frisée with salt and pepper and toss in a large bowl with two-thirds of the vinaigrette. Add the orange segments and toasted almonds and toss again. Divide the salad among 6 plates, drain the asparagus (discard the liquid), then portion the asparagus on top of the frisée. Drizzle the remaining vinaigrette over the asparagus, then garnish each plate with 3 anchovies.

Blood Orange Vinaigrette

2 teaspoons prepared mustard

1 teaspoon finely chopped fresh
oregano

1 teaspoon minced garlic

2 tablespoons fresh blood orange
juice

1 tablespoon red wine vinegar

3 tablespoons olive oil

Salt and freshly ground black
pepper

Blend the mustard, oregano, garlic, orange juice, and vinegar in a small bowl. Whisk in the olive oil. Season with salt and pepper to taste.

PREPARING ASPARAGUS

To trim asparagus, hold a stalk at the midpoint and the very bottom with the thumb and index fingers of both hands. Bend the stalk until it snaps. The place where it naturally snaps will leave you with a woody, tough part (which you can discard) and a top that's sweet and tender. This is how you achieve perfection with asparagus. To make your asparagus even more tender, remove the outer layer of skin on the stalk: Lay the stem down on a cutting board and use a vegetable peeler or small paring knife to peel off the very outer layer, turning the stem over and working lengthwise from bottom to tip.

Saffron-Braised Squid with Ragoût of White Beans, Chorizo, and Rosemary

This is one of my longtime favorite Spanish stews. L'Espalier often has it on the menu in one way or another. I've been making this dish for almost 20 years. It's rich and memorable, and the contrasting sweetness of the squid and acidity of the tomatoes gives you a mouthful of joy. Really.

2 tablespoons olive oil

1 medium-size yellow onion, diced

4 garlic cloves, minced

1 leek, split in half, washed (page 195), and diced

2 celery stalks, diced

One 4-ounce can tomato paste

3 plum tomatoes, peeled (page 123), seeded, and chopped

¼ teaspoon ground allspice

¼ teaspoon ground cumin

¼ teaspoon ground cinnamon

1 whole clove

1 bay leaf

2 cups rosé

1 cup white beans, soaked, or one 16-ounce can cannellini beans, drained

2 cups vegetable broth

1 Heat a large pot over medium-high heat. Add the oil. When the oil is hot, add the onion and cook until translucent, about 3 minutes. Add the garlic and stir with a wooden spoon for 1 minute. Add the leek and celery and cook for 4 minutes. Add the tomato paste and tomatoes and stir. Add the allspice, cumin, cinnamon, clove, and bay leaf. Reduce the heat to low and cover. Cook for 8 minutes, stirring occasionally.

2 Uncover, turn the heat up to medium, and add the wine. Cook for 4 to 5 minutes, or until the liquid is reduced by one-third. Add the beans and the broth and reduce the heat to low. Cover and cook for 30 minutes, or until the beans are tender.

(continued)

1 pound cleaned squid, tentacles detached and cut if needed, body cut into ¼-inch-thick rings

1 link Spanish (smoked) chorizo, sliced in half lengthwise and cut into ¼-inch cubes

2 teaspoons saffron

2 sprigs fresh rosemary, needles removed and minced

1 tablespoon sherry vinegar

Salt and freshly ground black pepper

Manchego cheese for grating (optional)

Garlic croutons (optional; below)

3 Uncover the pot and turn the heat up to medium. Add the squid rings and tentacles and cook for 18 minutes, or until the squid is tender. Add the chorizo and cook for 5 minutes. Add the saffron, rosemary, and vinegar—and don't cook for more than 1 minute longer. Season with salt and pepper and serve immediately. Ladle into bowls, and, if desired, grate manchego cheese over each bowl and serve with garlic croutons.

GARLIC CROUTONS

To make garlic-rubbed croutons, crush 2 garlic cloves. Combine the garlic in a bowl with 1 teaspoon salt, 2 tablespoons olive oil, ¼ teaspoon freshly ground black pepper, and ¼ teaspoon paprika. Cut a baguette into twelve ½-inch-thick slices and toss them in the garlic mixture until coated. Lay the bread on a baking sheet and bake at 375°F for 8 minutes, or until just golden brown but still chewy.

Rioja-Roasted Lamb with Chickpeas, Black Olives, and Escarole

I love lamb shanks. They are so sweet and tender. This is a great dish to start preparing in the early afternoon—then just put it in the oven and let it cook. Your house will smell amazing. Make sure you have more than one bottle of wine to serve your guests with this dish. You'll all be very happy and festive while enjoying it, and you won't want the party to stop.

2 teaspoons dried oregano

1 teaspoon dried thyme

1 teaspoon *piment d'Espelette* or ground sweet pimiento pepper

2 teaspoons garlic powder

3 lamb shanks (about 2 pounds total)

4 slices smoked bacon, chopped

2 yellow onions, diced

5 garlic cloves, minced

2 carrots, peeled and diced

3 celery stalks, peeled and diced

1 bottle Rioja

1 quart chicken broth

2 sprigs fresh thyme

1 bay leaf

1 sprig fresh oregano

1 Combine the oregano, dried thyme, *piment d'Espelette*, and garlic powder in a large bowl. Place the lamb shanks in the bowl and rub them evenly with the spice mixture. Cover and refrigerate for at least 2 hours and up to overnight.

2 Remove the shanks from the refrigerator at least 1 hour before cooking. Preheat the oven to 350°F.

3 Place a large ovenproof skillet over medium heat. Add the bacon and cook until the fat has been rendered, about 5 minutes. Turn the heat up to medium-high and add the shanks. Sear until golden brown on all sides, about 3 minutes per side. Reduce the heat to medium, add the onions, and cook until translucent, about 3 minutes. Add the garlic and cook for 2 minutes. Add the carrots and celery, cover, and cook for 10 minutes. Uncover, add the wine, and bring to a simmer. Add the broth, fresh thyme, bay leaf, and oregano and bring back to a simmer.

(continued)

1 cup dried chickpeas, soaked overnight, or one 16-ounce can chickpeas, drained

1 cup pitted and chopped kalamata olives

1 head escarole, chopped

2 roasted red peppers (page 161)

Salt and freshly ground black pepper

4 Cover and roast the lamb in the oven for 1 hour. Remove from the oven, add the chickpeas, and return to the oven for 30 more minutes. Remove from the oven and stir in the olives, escarole, and red peppers. Season with salt and pepper to taste before serving.

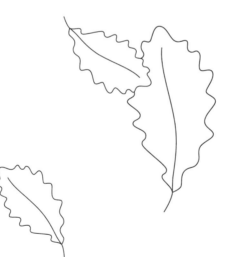

Rice Pudding with Raisins and Pine Nuts

Rice pudding is a crowd pleaser every time. Serve it and people will relax and linger over it and feel warm and fuzzy. It's a great way to finish off a welcoming evening of Spanish food and wine.

½ cup sultanas or golden raisins

3 tablespoons brandy

1 cup short-grain white rice (unrinsed)

1 cup sugar

4¼ cups milk

¼ teaspoon pure vanilla extract

1 cinnamon stick

¼ cup pine nuts

Ground cinnamon for dusting

1 Place the sultanas in a small bowl and soak them in the brandy for at least 10 minutes or up to 1 day. Place the rice, sugar, and milk in a medium-size saucepan over medium heat. Add the vanilla and the cinnamon stick. When the milk starts to boil, reduce the heat to very low and continue to cook, stirring occasionally to keep the rice from sticking, for 25 to 30 minutes, or until the rice is tender.

2 Stir the brandy-soaked sultanas and the pine nuts into the rice. Remove the pan from the heat and remove the cinnamon stick. Divide the pudding among 6 serving dishes and let cool for at least 15 minutes or up to 1 hour. Sprinkle with a scant dusting of cinnamon and serve at room temperature or chilled.

AUTUMN MUSHROOM DINNER

Foraging mushrooms is something I do every fall, and I've taught my team at the restaurant and my family how to do it. It's like a treasure hunt. When we forage as a group we always make dinner from the mushrooms we find. The scent of mushrooms always makes me think of the New England woods in the fall. Mushrooms go beautifully with all kinds of foods, absorbing flavors while lending their own subtle, sexy depth, so it's fun to create a dinner totally inspired by mushrooms.

MENU

& pairings

↓

 +

PAIRINGS

**Truffled Leek Mousse
with Cèpe Vinaigrette**

1

**1999 Westport Rivers,
"Cuvée L'Espalier," Brut,
Westport, Massachusetts**

**Seared Scallops
with Shiitake Nage**

2

**2004 Sigalas,
Assyrtiko, Santorini,
Greece**

**Civet of Rabbit
with Chanterelles
and Spaetzle**

3

**2002 Derain, "Le Ban,"
Saint-Aubin, Burgundy,
France**

**Bittersweet Chocolate Terrine
with Warm Pumpkin Sauce
and Shaved Black Truffle**

4

**1999 Traginer,
"Mise Tardive,"
Banyuls, France**

WINE 🍾 NOTES

↓

1ST PAIRING **TRUFFLED LEEK MOUSSE WITH CÈPE VINAIGRETTE**
SERVED WITH → 1999 WESTPORT RIVERS, "CUVÉE L'ESPALIER," BRUT, WESTPORT, MASSACHUSETTS

The mousse with truffles makes for a rich first course, and the dry, crisp bubbles of this sparkling wine, which Westport Rivers bottles for L'Espalier (though they make similar wines that are widely available), cuts right through that to cleanse the palate. Dry bubbles are the way to go here.

2ND PAIRING **SEARED SCALLOPS WITH SHIITAKE NAGE**
SERVED WITH → 2004 SIGALAS, ASSYRTIKO, SANTORINI, GREECE

In Santorini this ancient grape variety is never grown far from the coast, so the wine has a zippy salinity that's perfect with seafood, and also great with mushrooms. Another crisp white, like a snappy Pinot Grigio, would also be nice with this dish.

3RD PAIRING **CIVET OF RABBIT WITH CHANTERELLES AND SPAETZLE**
SERVED WITH → 2002 DERAIN, "LE BAN," SAINT-AUBIN, BURGUNDY, FRANCE

This part of Burgundy is better known for its white wines, but it also produces this ter-rific—and organic—Pinot Noir, which showcases the pure flavor of the grapes: earthy and spicy, with the essence of red berries. Pinot Noir is a good choice when serving rabbit, whose flavor is delicate and could be overpowered by a more intense wine.

4TH PAIRING **BITTERSWEET CHOCOLATE TERRINE WITH WARM PUMPKIN SAUCE AND SHAVED BLACK TRUFFLE**
SERVED WITH → 1999 TRAGINER, "MISE TARDIVE," BANYULS, FRANCE

A sweet dessert wine from the southwest part of France, this tastes similar to port and is heavenly served with chocolate. Port is a natural alternative here.

Truffled Leek Mousse with Cèpe Vinaigrette

Cèpes (pronounced "seps") are the French version of Italian porcini mushrooms. Their flavor is fantastic with truffles and leeks. I think people should cook with leeks more often. They can be used in almost any preparation. They have a sweet onion flavor that's light on the palate and they pick up other flavors easily. You might not immediately know there are leeks in a dish, but they round it out and give subtle depth.

4 large leeks, washed (page 195)

2 marinated white anchovies

¼ pound chicken breast, chopped and refrigerated (very cold)

1 large egg, separated

1 teaspoon salt, plus more for seasoning the ramekins

¼ cup heavy cream

1 garlic clove, minced

Zest of 1 lemon

¼ teaspoon ground nutmeg

½ teaspoon freshly ground white pepper

1 teaspoon white truffle oil

¼ teaspoon cayenne pepper

1 tablespoon chopped black truffles (canned, jarred, or fresh)

2 tablespoons minced fresh chives

Butter for the ramekins

Freshly ground black pepper

6 cups field greens

Cèpe Vinaigrette (page 195)

1 Place the bowl and blade of a food processor in the freezer so they will be very cold.

2 Remove the dark green tops and outer layer of the leeks. Blanch the white parts of the leeks in salted water for 10 minutes, or until tender. Shock them in ice water, remove from the water, and place on paper towels to drain. Puree 2 of the blanched leeks with the white anchovies in the chilled food processor, remove the pureed mixture to a bowl, and set aside. Clean the bowl and blade of the food processor and place in the freezer to chill again. Dice 1 of the remaining blanched leeks and set aside. Reserve the fourth leek.

3 Place the cold chicken in the chilled food processor and puree until pasty. Add the egg white and salt while pureeing. When the egg white and salt are completely incorporated, add the egg yolk and continue pureeing. Add the heavy cream slowly as you continue to puree. Then add the pureed leek-anchovy mixture slowly, followed by the garlic, lemon zest, nutmeg, white pepper, white truffle oil, and cayenne pepper. Puree until well combined.

4 Transfer the mousse mixture to a large bowl. Fold in the black truffles, chives, and diced leek. Cover and refrigerate for 1 hour.

(continued)

5 Preheat the oven to 350°F. Butter six 4-ounce ramekins.

6 Separate the layers of the remaining blanched leek. Lay the individual leek layers across each other in the ramekins, covering the entire insides of the ramekins. Season with salt and pepper.

7 Evenly distribute the mousse among the ramekins. Fold the ends of the leek layers over the top of the mousse. Place the ramekins inside a roasting pan filled with enough hot water to reach halfway up the sides of the ramekins. Bake for 18 minutes, or until the internal temperature is 150°F on an instant-read thermometer. Remove from the oven and unmold the mousses onto the centers of 6 plates.

8 Arrange field greens loosely around each mousse and drizzle the mousse and greens with the vinaigrette.

Cèpe Vinaigrette

1 teaspoon vegetable oil

2 shallots, minced

1 large garlic clove, minced

4 ounces fresh cèpes, or ¾ ounce dried, reconstituted cèpes (page 91), thinly sliced

1 teaspoon chopped fresh tarragon

2 teaspoons champagne vinegar

3 tablespoons extra virgin olive oil

1 teaspoon prepared mustard

1 teaspoon fresh lemon juice

½ teaspoon Worcestershire sauce

¼ teaspoon freshly ground black pepper

Salt

1 Heat a medium-size sauté pan over medium heat. Add the vegetable oil. When hot, add the shallots. Cook for 2 minutes, stirring with a wooden spoon. Add the garlic and cook for 1 minute, stirring. Add the sliced cèpes, stir, and cover. Reduce the heat to low and cook for 10 minutes, stirring occasionally. Stir in the tarragon and remove from the heat.

2 In a small bowl, whisk together the vinegar, olive oil, mustard, lemon juice, Worcestershire sauce, pepper, and salt. Add the contents of the sauté pan and combine. Adjust the seasonings to taste before serving, if necessary.

WASHING LEEKS

The green parts of leeks tend to come with quite a bit of grit and sand. In this recipe you're using only the white part of the leek, but save the green part and use it for something else. To wash the green part, split it in half the long way and submerge it in tepid water for 10 minutes. Then use your fingers to make sure all the grit is detached. Remove the leek from the water, shake it dry, and slice.

Seared Scallops with Shiitake Nage

A nage is an aromatic broth, and here the fragrances of the mushrooms and scallops envelop you before you take your first bite. Try to find dry-pack scallops, not scallops bloated with phosphate-laced water. Lovage is an herb with strong celery flavor. It's great in broth or in spring rolls, stir-fries, flatbreads, or salads—and a little goes a long way. Sub in celery tops if you cannot find it. I like the aromatic quality of white pepper with the scallops, and with just about any seafood. It's great to have white peppercorns on hand in your kitchen, but if you don't, you can use black pepper here.

12 large sea scallops
(about 1¼ pounds)

1 tablespoon olive oil

¼ teaspoon ground fennel

Zest of 1 orange

Zest of 1 lemon

1 tablespoon chopped fresh
lovage

½ teaspoon cracked white
pepper

Salt

2 tablespoons peanut oil

1 Wash the scallops and remove their muscles if still attached. Soak in ice water for 1 minute. Remove and pat dry.

2 Make a marinade by combining the olive oil, fennel, orange and lemon zests, lovage, and white pepper in a large bowl. Toss the scallops with the marinade, cover, and refrigerate for 2 hours or overnight.

3 Preheat the oven to 400°F.

4 Remove the scallops from the marinade and dust them with salt. Heat a medium-size ovenproof sauté pan over medium-high heat. Add the peanut oil. When the oil is hot, add the scallops to the pan and cook for 30 seconds on one side. Do not turn them.

5 Transfer the pan to the oven and cook for 4 to 5 minutes. Be careful not to over-cook—the scallops shouldn't spring back if you press them in the center. Remove the pan from the oven, turn the scallops over, and let them stand in the pan for 4 minutes before serving. Serve in bowls with Shiitake Nage (recipe follows) ladled on top.

Shiitake Nage

2 tablespoons butter

5 shallots, minced

3 garlic cloves, minced

¼ teaspoon ground cinnamon

½ teaspoon ground fennel, or
1 tablespoon chopped fresh
fennel tops

4 ounces shiitake mushrooms,
stemmed and thinly sliced

2 tablespoons Madeira

½ cup crisp white wine (such as
Sancerre)

1 cup vegetable broth

¼ cup heavy cream

1 teaspoon fresh lemon juice

1 teaspoon chopped fresh
tarragon

1 teaspoon chopped fresh lovage

Salt and freshly ground black
pepper

1 Heat a medium-size saucepan over medium heat. Add the butter to the pan, and when the butter is melted, add the shallots. Stir with a wooden spoon until the shallots are golden brown on their edges, 4 to 5 minutes. Add the garlic and cook for 1 minute. Add the cinnamon and fennel and cook for 1 minute. Add the shiitakes and cook for 2 minutes. Cover, reduce the heat to low, and cook for 4 more minutes.

2 Uncover and turn the heat up to medium. Add the Madeira and cook for 1 minute, or until absorbed. Add the white wine and bring to a simmer for 3 minutes. Add the broth and cream and bring to a simmer for 4 minutes.

3 Add the lemon juice, tarragon, lovage, salt, and pepper and cook for 1 more minute.

Civet of Rabbit with Chanterelles and Spaetzle

Rabbit has a rich, sweet flavor that is somewhat neutral, so it plays well off of other flavors. I grew up eating rabbit in the fall, so I always associate it with that time of year. In fact, mushroom foragers often hunt rabbit and hare in the fall when they're out in search of mushrooms. Rabbit with mushrooms is a longtime favorite combination at L'Espalier. Ask your butcher to cut up the rabbit for you.

2 garlic cloves, crushed

2 teaspoons dried basil

1 teaspoon dried thyme

1 teaspoon ground coriander

½ teaspoon ground allspice

12 ounces rabbit (2 hind legs and 2 loins)

3 large tomatoes, peeled (page 123), cut in half, and seeded

1 tablespoon balsamic vinegar

2 tablespoons olive oil

2 tablespoons lard or olive oil

Salt

5 shallots, sliced

2 garlic cloves, minced

8 ounces chanterelle or other wild mushrooms, sliced in half

1 cup red wine

½ cup chicken broth

One 14-ounce can artichoke hearts, drained and rinsed

2 teaspoons dried rosemary

1 Make a dry rub by combining the crushed garlic, 1 teaspoon of the basil, the thyme, coriander, and allspice. Rub it all over the rabbit and let stand, covered, in the refrigerator for 3 hours or up to overnight. Remove the rabbit from the refrigerator at least 1 hour before cooking.

2 Preheat the oven to 400°F.

3 Toss the tomatoes with the vinegar, olive oil, and the remaining 1 teaspoon basil in a nonreactive baking dish and bake for 40 minutes. Remove the tomatoes from the oven, let cool, chop coarsely, and set aside.

4 Heat a medium-size ovenproof skillet over high heat. Add the lard to the pan and lightly salt the rabbit. When the lard has melted, add the rabbit to the pan and cook for 4 minutes, browning lightly. Remove the loins and reserve. Cover the skillet and transfer it to the oven. Reduce the oven temperature to 350°F.

5 Cook the rabbit for 15 minutes, remove from the oven, and uncover. Turn the legs and place the skillet on the stovetop over medium heat. Add the shallots, minced garlic, and chanterelles and cook for 3 to 4 minutes, stirring with a wooden spoon.

Add the red wine and cook for 3 to 4 minutes. Add the chicken broth and bring to a simmer, then add the artichoke hearts, chopped cooked tomatoes, and rosemary. Cover the skillet, return it to the oven, and cook for 15 minutes.

6 Return the rabbit loins to the skillet and cook for another 5 minutes. Remove the skillet from the oven and place it on the stovetop over medium heat. Remove the legs and loins from the pan, slice the meat, and return it to the pan. Let simmer for 4 minutes. Serve the rabbit with the vegetables and braising liquid, with Spaetzle (recipe follows) on the side. Or serve the Spaetzle topped with the rabbit, vegetables, and braising liquid.

Spaetzle

1²/₃ cups all-purpose flour

6 tablespoons milk

2 large eggs

1 tablespoon whole-grain mustard

½ teaspoon salt

¼ teaspoon freshly ground black pepper

1 In a medium-size bowl, make a dough by combining the flour, milk, eggs, mustard, salt, and pepper.

2 Bring a medium-size pot of salted water to a boil. Press the spaetzle dough through a colander with ¼-inch-diameter holes directly into the boiling water. Cook for 2 minutes. Drain well and serve.

Bittersweet Chocolate Terrine with Warm Pumpkin Sauce and Shaved Black Truffle

Chocolate and pumpkin is a surprising combination, and it's delicious and perfect for a fall dinner. Shaved black truffle on top lends sophistication and earthiness to this dessert, but you don't absolutely need it if you can't find or don't want to purchase black truffles.

1 tablespoon vegetable oil

14 ounces bittersweet chocolate, chopped

1 cup (2 sticks) butter

4 large eggs, separated

5 large egg yolks

1¼ cups confectioners' sugar

½ cup unsweetened cocoa powder

1 tablespoon granulated sugar

½ cup heavy cream

One 2-ounce fresh or canned black truffle

1   Brush a 1-quart terrine mold with the vegetable oil, then press a layer of plastic wrap into the mold, being sure to press the plastic wrap evenly against the inside of the mold and allowing enough extra to hang over the sides of the mold. Set aside.

2   Place the chopped chocolate and butter in a large heatproof mixing bowl and gently melt the chocolate and butter over a saucepan of hot water (make sure the water is only hot, not quite simmering), stirring occasionally. When the chocolate and butter are completely melted, remove the bowl from the heat and let cool just until the mixture is warm to the touch.

3   Stir in the 9 egg yolks, then sift in the confectioners' sugar and cocoa powder. In a medium-size bowl, beat the 4 egg whites and granulated sugar with an electric mixer until soft peaks form. Fold into the chocolate mixture.

4 In a separate medium-size bowl, beat the heavy cream with an electric mixer until soft peaks form. Fold into the chocolate mixture. Pour the mixture into the prepared terrine mold, cover with plastic wrap, and refrigerate until completely set, about 2 hours.

5 Remove the terrine from the refrigerator, remove the plastic wrap, invert the terrine onto a platter, and unmold. Slice the terrine, drizzle with Warm Pumpkin Sauce (recipe follows), and shave the black truffle over the warm sauce.

Note: This terrine contains raw eggs, and it should not be served to anyone with a compromised immune system.

Warm Pumpkin Sauce

2 cups diced pumpkin (below)

1/3 cup sugar

6 tablespoons heavy cream

3 tablespoons butter, cut into pieces

2 tablespoons maple syrup

2 tablespoons white wine

1/4 teaspoon ground cinnamon

1/2 teaspoon pure vanilla extract

1 Combine the pumpkin, sugar, cream, butter, maple syrup, wine, cinnamon, and vanilla in a medium-size saucepan. Bring to a light simmer over medium heat, then reduce the heat to low, cover, and let cook for 30 minutes, or until the pumpkin is completely tender and falling apart.

2 Puree in a blender or food processor until smooth. Serve warm.

CUTTING FRESH PUMPKIN

Use a very sharp knife to cut off both ends, then carve around the outside of the pumpkin, removing the skin with the knife. When all the skin is removed, cut the pumpkin in half vertically, remove the seeds, and dice the flesh.

MEASUREMENT EQUIVALENTS

Please note that all conversions are approximate.

Liquid Conversions

U.S.	IMPERIAL	METRIC
1 tsp		5 ml
1 tbs	½ fl oz	15 ml
2 tbs	1 fl oz	30 ml
3 tbs	1½ fl oz	45 ml
¼ cup	2 fl oz	60 ml
⅓ cup	2½ fl oz	75 ml
⅓ cup + 1 tbs	3 fl oz	90 ml
⅓ cup + 2 tbs	3½ fl oz	100 ml
½ cup	4 fl oz	120 ml
⅔ cup	5 fl oz	150 ml
¾ cup	6 fl oz	180 ml
¾ cup + 2 tbs	7 fl oz	200 ml
1 cup	8 fl oz	240 ml
1 cup + 2 tbs	9 fl oz	275 ml
1¼ cups	10 fl oz	300 ml
1⅓ cups	11 fl oz	325 ml
1½ cups	12 fl oz	350 ml
1⅔ cups	13 fl oz	375 ml
1¾ cups	14 fl oz	400 ml
1¾ cups + 2 tbs	15 fl oz	450 ml
2 cups (1 pint)	16 fl oz	475 ml
2½ cups	20 fl oz	600 ml
3 cups	24 fl oz	720 ml
4 cups (1 quart)	32 fl oz	945 ml
		(1,000 ml is 1 liter)

Weight Conversions

U.S./U.K.	METRIC
½ oz	14 g
1 oz	28 g
1½ oz	43 g
2 oz	57 g
2½ oz	71 g
3 oz	85 g
3½ oz	100 g
4 oz	113 g
5 oz	142 g
6 oz	170 g
7 oz	200 g
8 oz	227 g
9 oz	255 g
10 oz	284 g
11 oz	312 g
12 oz	340 g
13 oz	368 g
14 oz	400 g
15 oz	425 g
1 lb	454 g

Oven Temperature Conversions

°F	GAS MARK	°C
250	½	120
275	1	140
300	2	150
325	3	165
350	4	180
375	5	190
400	6	200
425	7	220
450	8	230
475	9	240
500	10	260
550	Broil	290

INDEX